CREATING FANTASY POLYMER CLAY CHARACTERS

Step-by-step trolls, wizards, dragons, knights, skeletons, Santa, and more!

Dinko Tilov

GLOUCESTER MASSACHUSETTS

QUARRY BOOKS

First published in the United States of America by
Quarry Books, an imprint of
Rockport Publishers, Inc.
33 Commercial Street
Gloucester, Massachusetts 01930-5089
Telephone: (978) 282-9590
Fax: (978) 283-2742
www.rockpub.com

Library of Congress Cataloging-in-Publication Data
Tilov, Dinko.
   Creating fantasy polymer clay characters : step-by-step trolls, wizards, dragons, knights, skeletons, Santa, and more! : making fantasy polymer characters / by Dinko Tilov.
      p.   cm.
   ISBN 1-59253-020-6 (pbk.)
   1. Polymer clay craft. I. Title.
TT297.T574 2004
731.4'2—dc22   2003020796

ISBN 1-59253-020-6

10 9 8 7 6 5 4 3

Design: Bob's Your Uncle
Cover Art and Design: Jerrod Janakus

Printed in Singapore

CONTENTS

INTRODUCTION

We have all seen fantasy characters and are familiar with their characteristics. Examples are everywhere—in movies, books, and games. Trolls, goblins, elves, wizards. Someone must be able to see these critters, because they are able to re-create them in great detail. A place exists where you too can see these magical critters, a place where cameras do not work and everybody brings back a different image.

This place is called your imagination, and we want to take you there so that you can conjure your own fantasy characters. This book will guide you if you follow the step-by-step instructions, or it can accompany you if you decide to stray a little from the path. It is a win-win situation; whether you adhere to or vary the project instructions, you can't mess up.

The steps in this book cover technical aspects of making a character, such as how to make a nose with your fingers, as well as creative aspects, such as: why one should bother to make a nose at all? And if so, should it be pointy or chipped? The projects are designed to offer you guidance on the former and suggestions on the latter. You do not need previous experience in sculpting or polymer clay to complete the projects—information on the medium, the tools, and how to use them together is provided.

You can skip straight to a project of your choice without having completed those before it. A certain evolution in difficulty exists, however, as you progress from the front of the book toward the back, so keep that in mind.

You will discover new ways to use all the little odds and ends lying around in drawers—safety pins, buttons, broken pens, cheap jewelry, kitsch souvenirs, travel trinkets. You can even use dead light bulbs to make accessories for your fantasy characters.

To sum up: You don't need any special training to make one of these critters because it is all explained—and you just cannot get a fantasy character wrong. In addition, you'll get a jump on spring cleaning by making magic crystals out of your old marbles.

Hold on to these reassuring thoughts and happy claying! Maybe you will bring back a character no one has ever seen before....

Your fellow critter-maker,
Dinko Tilov

What Is Polymer Clay?

Polymer clay is a synthetic modeling material that you can bake, or cure, in an oven. It comes in different brands and colors and can be sculpted, carved, textured, sanded, and painted. Polymer clay does not create a mess and does not require any special setup or equipment. These properties make this versatile medium very accessible to beginners, as well as a first choice for sculpting small characters. Polymer clay is easy to work with and allows you to concentrate on the process of creation rather than on struggling with the material.

Finding Polymer Clay Tools and Supplies

You can find polymer clay tools and supplies in arts and crafts stores, or you can order them online.

Please see the Resources section at the back of this book for more information.

The Wrong Tool for the Right Job

The philosophy of this book is that you shouldn't let a shortage of the *right* polymer clay or the *right* tools stop you. To illustrate this point, I have used polymer clays ranging from Fimo Soft to Super Sculpey and everything from a safety pin to a clay shaper as tools for the projects in this book. You should feel free to improvise. Personally, I prefer, and recommend, the Premo Sculpey brand of clay for its nice finish and sturdiness after baking. As a rule of thumb, try to avoid clays that are too soft or sticky for your taste. The brand of clay, its color, and its quantity should not be obstacles to sculpting success. The color schemes in the projects are only a suggestion, and it is up to you whether a Little Red Riding Hood will wear a bright yellow hat or not.

The quantities of clay needed, which are stated in the beginning of each project, are a rough estimate and always give you the maximum amount you would need. This method avoids impractical measurement units, such as $1/231$ block of clay, and helps you develop a sense of proportion.

As for tools, I recommend the use of *clay shapers*, because their rubbery tips are excellent for manipulating the clay. The tapered-point and the cup-round clay shapers in particular are used for most of the projects in this book. Alternatively, you can use a *cuticle pusher*, a common manicure tool, instead of a clay shaper. This tool is also the best choice for hard clays (or older clays), for which the soft tip of the shaper does not work well. Do not hesitate to experiment with other tools that seem to fulfill the same function as a clay shaper or a cuticle pusher; there is no tool that cannot be switched for something else—except for your hands, of course.

All the previously mentioned standard tools and supplies can be found online or in arts and crafts stores. For more information, see the Resources section in the back of this book.

How to Read the Instructions

The project instructions in this book are designed to first and foremost give you a *visual* idea of how a critter is made. While working, keep in mind that each step is not an isolated move, but comes in the continuity of what has already been done in the previous step and what will be done in the next one. To make the most out of the visual instructions for each step, try to take a quick look at the one before it and the one after it. That way you do not run risks such as making an excessively large earlobe that blocks a sideburn that needs to make its way onto the cheek of an Elvis impersonator.

How to Hold a Critter

Many of the pictures in this book do not show how you should hold a critter while working on it. A goofy head sitting by itself in the middle of a light blue desert with a clay shaper stuck in its ear will not be an uncommon sight. However, you will often need to exert counterpressure to a certain manipulation or simply hold a bit of clay to have better access to the surface on which you are working.

Generally, you should hold a critter like you would hold a baby—you have to support the bottom (the heavier part that is dragging down the whole) and you have to make sure its head doesn't come off. The easiest way to do this is to keep your thumb on the bottom and your fingers or fingertips on the back (which is usually plain and where there is nothing to ruin).

Baking

The last and often most important step of making a polymer clay character is baking. You can use either an electric or a gas oven to bake polymer clay. A convection oven is best because the fan inside helps the hot air circulate evenly around the critter. When baking, always follow the specific clay manufacturer's instructions on the package—they will provide the basics. The following tips are additional hints that may save you some trial and error:

- One of the main objectives when baking is to preserve the shapes you have created. Often when you put a character in the oven, it might lean to one side (or stick its nose to the baking tray, just out of curiosity). To avoid this problem, make tin foil props.

- Also use tin foil to cover your creatures so that they don't change color too much—prolonged, unprotected exposure of a critter to oven heat may lead to crisp, caramel-colored formations on their soft polymer-clay skin.

- Do not exceed the baking temperature indicated for the brand of clay you are using. As long as you bake at the right temperature, the critter will get stronger and stronger with every additional minute of baking and won't burn. Generally, bigger critters like to spend more time in the oven.

- Keep in mind that when you turn the oven dial to 275°F (135°C), the temperature inside the oven is not necessarily 275°F. Ovens are not exactly the sharpest NASA gear. Ideally, try to find an oven thermometer to measure the actual temperature, thus ensuring the safety of your critters. If you don't have a thermometer or if you are baking for the first time in an oven, it is always a good idea to give a small chunk of clay a test ride before baking your day's work. Check on the critter every now and then to make sure everything is all right.

- Be careful when you take critters out of the oven—they will be quite fragile until they cool. If you overbake a critter, do not inhale the fumes and immediately air out the room. Remember, you can always make a better one.

- You can bake an underbaked critter over and over again without damaging the clay as long as you bake at the right temperature. This is very useful for fixing critters—you can just attach a missing arm and cure the whole critter one more time.

- When making a more complicated character, you might find it helpful to bake the critter midway through the process and then continue working on a more solid structure.

You will be referred back to this basic "baking" section at the end of each lesson, so keep this section handy until you have become experienced with your baking methods.

This grinning bird, looking up, settled over his gigantic bird feet, teeth gleaming through his smile, is a perfect starting project, particularly if you are completely new to working with clay. Making the bird, fun in itself, is also useful practice in the essential skills that you will need for the rest of the projects in this book such as: making basic shapes and learning how to work on a specific area of a critter without ruining the rest of it.

The color scheme should follow this one guideline: use two well-contrasting colors—one for the fluffy parts (the body, the wigs, and the tail) and one for the bony parts (the beak and legs).

The size of the bird doesn't matter, as long as its proportions make sense. The bird shown here is less than 1" (2.5 cm) tall. (But don't underestimate him!)

¼ **block yellow clay (we used Sculpey Premo)**

½ **block green clay**

⅛ **block white or glow-in-the-dark clay**

⅛ **block orange clay**

⅛ **block black clay**

Safety pin

Taped-point clay shaper

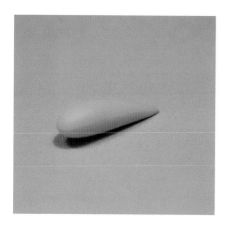

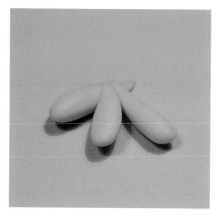

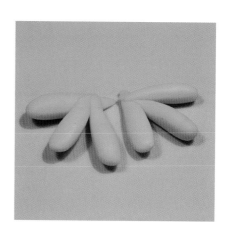

1 A bird is built the way a house is built, from bottom to top, so we will start with the feet. The foot of an average bird consists of three toes. To make a toe, roll a small ball of clay between your index finger and thumb until it becomes oblong. Make the back end slightly sharper by exerting a little bit more pressure while rolling. The pointed end will go under the bird, and the round end will be the tip of the toe. That way, the bird will have nice, chubby toes instead of scary claws.

2 Continue with the other two toes, and stick the pointy ends firmly on top of one another. Make sure to sufficiently overlap the toes, so that they will provide a firm, solid base once the bird is cooked. The outside toes should form a 90-degree (right) angle so that the bird can stand firmly on his feet.

3 Repeat the procedure to make a second foot. Make sure to include the same number of toes in each foot—it is considered to be good taste.

4 Next, create an egg shape, which will become the body of the bird. Roll a ball of clay between the palms of your hands, gently squeezing your palms toward the end, while still rolling, to achieve an egglike shape. Stick the body firmly to the feet. Remember that the body keeps the feet together, so if you want to have a solid bird, you'll need to apply a little pressure. Be careful not to disfigure the oval shape of the egg while pressing.

5 The bird's mouth is made from a triangular piece of clay. Make a small, flat triangle with equal-length sides. Flatten one point of the triangle to make it slightly thinner. This end will be the tip of the beak.

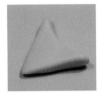

6 Pull the other two points in opposite directions, and curve the side between them. This side of the beak will be fastened to the body, so it should roughly follow the curves of the bird's body.

8 This step, where you first use the safety pin, involves separating the upper jaw from the lower one. Stick the pin into the beak where the curved part starts, and carefully pull toward the cheeks. Be careful not to pull too hard—you want to leave the jaws joined.

7 From this point on, working on the beak will be easier if you attach it to the body of the bird. Stick the beak to the body horizontally. Whether you will make a highbrow or a lowbrow bird depends on how high on the body you place the beak. Putting it in the upper part leads to a lowbrow bird with a belly. Gently push the top of the beak down. (This feature of the bird is probably the only one that bears resemblance to an eagle.)

9 Use the safety pin again to widen the distance between the jaws. Try to make a hole in a sideways, teardrop shape. You will put the teeth in this space.

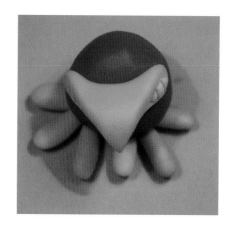

🔺 **10** Fill the holes with white polymer clay. If you want your feathered songster to have bad teeth you can, of course, use yellowish clay. You can also put a cigar in the bird's mouth instead or even make him stick out his tongue. But teeth…teeth are classic.

🔺 **11** Use the safety pin to divide the white polymer clay into individual teeth. Be careful not to touch the beak. Repeatedly rock the tip of the pin back and forth rather than just drawing it straight from one jaw to the other to avoid creating a "wake" of clay around the pin and ultimately ruining the shapes you previously created.

🔺 **12** Here is a bird's eye view of the bird.

🔺 **13** Roll out two small balls of white polymer clay for the eyeballs. For the eyelids, roll out two colored balls approximately the same size and a color darker than the beak. Squash the colored balls flat. Don't make perfect spheres, though. You want a slightly elliptical shape, so start with an elongated ball. Wrap the ellipses around the eyeballs, so that they cover half of the circumference and the rim sticks out, sort of like a baseball cap. You can see the making of the eyes in the photo above.

▲ ▶ **14** Add the eyes to the body of the bird. Stick them to the egg and to the beak at the same time. The beak and the eyes form the face of the bird, so make sure to set them close together.

▲ **15** Next, you need to make wings for your bird. Make them by squeezing two small balls into disks.

▲ **17** Make the tail just like you made the feet, but use the same color clay that you used to make the body. Then, flatten the oblong rolls to resemble feathers. The number of feathers, just like the number of toes, can vary indefinitely.

▲ **16** Stick one rounded end of the wing to the body at the height of the beak. Slightly spread the lower, loose end of a wing away from the body. Repeat this procedure to attach the other wing.

▲ **18** Attach the tail to the bottom of the bird.

19 Turn the bird around. Now you need to give it eyes that see, a nose to breathe with, and a belly button. (Have you been wondering what an ordinary bird is doing in a book of fantasy characters? Well, it is the belly button that merits his inclusion.)

Using the safety pin, poke two deep holes into the eyes, one in the belly, and two on top of the beak. For the nostrils, pull a little bit to the side—the holes don't need to be perfectly round. Also, roll out two tiny strips of black clay, and put them on top of the eyelids to be the eyebrows.

Where to put the hole on the eyeball is a very important decision. Here are a few of the possible options:

MAKING EYES

The fact that we made a hole to create eyes and didn't just add a tiny black speck of clay is important. A small black spot is perceived the same way from any angle that you look at it. Because of this, the eye looks artificial. A hole, on the contrary, has depth and direction. In addition, only a limited number of angles provide the impression that your eyes and those of the bird lock, which gives the creature more character.

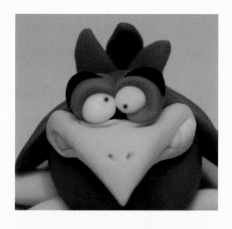

Dizzy ▶

◀ Looking left

Normal ▶

◀ Stunned

20 Here, the bird is looking up. Because it is a tiny creature, looking up is the easiest way for it to make eye contact with whoever is looking at it. That way the bird becomes more interactive and doesn't just sit there.

22 Use the tapered-point clay shaper to blend the cheeks with the rest of the beak.

Then, bake the bird following the clay manufacturer's instructions and let it cool. For more tips see the baking section in the beginning of this book.

21 The bird looks finished, but one final step remains—you can make it look cheekier. How? Just add cheeks. Use the same shape you made for the toes, only shorter and sharp at both ends. Then bend it as shown, and add it to the finished beak.

Congratulations—you have completed the project. By changing the color and the shape of the different parts, you can create any bird, from a penguin to a pelican. The small bits that you change make the personality of the creature. See the following page for more variations you can try.

TIP

White or Glow-in-the-Dark?

When you make the eyes and teeth, use glow-in-the dark clay instead of plain white polymer clay. The typical white is too white, and eyes and teeth usually have some translucency to them. Glow-in-the-dark clay not only lacks that undesirable opaqueness, but it also gives your creatures life after dark. For the best night results, after you have baked your bird, use a safety pin to fill the eyeholes with raw black polymer clay. Then turn the lights off, and observe.

Variation Ideas

Bird with an Extravagant Tail
The fellow is also sticking out his tongue.

Penguin

Make the penguin following the basic principles of the bird project. The only innovation is the white belly, made in the same way we made the wings and the feet.

A tip on how to make the penguin feet: After using the clay shaper, squeeze the toes with your fingers to flatten them.

Scared bird

The goal of this project is to teach you how to make a basic rabbit. Once you master that skill, the transition to an Easter Bunny will be quite easy—you only have to put an Easter egg in the rabbit's hands.

The Easter Bunny will be made in a somewhat different order that the bird. We start with the body and add the arms and legs later.

MATERIALS

1 block light blue clay
¼ block yellow clay
¼ block orange clay
⅛ block purple clay
⅛ block glow-in-the-dark clay
⅛ block pink clay
¼ block red clay

TOOLS

Needle or safety pin
Tapered-point clay shaper
Cup-round clay shaper

1 Using a piece of blue polymer clay and the palms of your hands, roll a ball approximately 1½" (3.8 cm) in diameter. Don't worry about making a perfect sphere —first, it would take too much time, and second, we don't need that level of precision. To make a character with a lot of character, we are counting on a combination of shapes that are often imperfect.

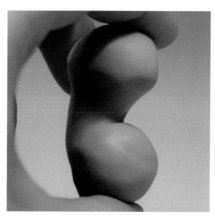

2 In this step hold the ball by the "equator" between your thumb and middle finger, and, by rolling back and forth, make it look like an apple core. Then gently smooth all edges until the shape starts looking more like an hourglass or an "8."

3 If you paid attention to the imperfection argument from the first step, by now one of the two ends should be slightly bigger than the other. This bigger end will be the torso of the rabbit, whereas the smaller end will be his head. Slightly bend the torso of the future Easter Bunny forward—the direction in which the belly is rounder and where the face of the critter will be.

Note: Stick the rabbit's bottom to the work surface until it flattens, and leave it there, as shown in step two. The figure should be able to stand without any props. Do not be alarmed if it is unstable, because we will add legs and a tail later, which will serve as additional support. This step is necessary because the upright position will be natural for the rabbit, which means that the "8" won't be flattened and distorted as it might be if just leave it lying, like an ∞.

4 Make a canoe shape out of the same color clay you used for the body. A canoe shape is flat on the surface, round on the bottom, and tapers off toward the ends. The canoe will be one of the ears. It should be about as long as the head/torso is tall.

Long ears are probably the most characteristic element of a rabbit, along with the small tail and the teeth. Even if you choose to ignore most of these instructions, as long as you give any critter long ears, two prominent teeth, and a tiny round tail, chances are you will end up with a rabbit. Once you practice here, you can go back and test this hypothesis on the bird for some interesting results.

5 It's time to make the soft part of the rabbit's fur. I have used a 50-50 mix of orange and yellow clay to create the rabbit color. (To mix colors, mush two pieces of different-colored clay together until they are completely blended into a new color.) Much in the same way you made the bird's toes, roll out a long worm of clay, with two sharp ends this time.

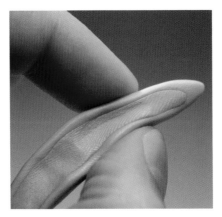

6 Flatten the clay worm into a tapeworm. Then put it on top of the flat surface of the canoe shape. Press firmly so that the yellow clay sinks in the blue one. The whole ear might flatten a little bit, but that is nothing to worry about.

7 Gently bend the ear until the blue rim comes slightly forward, as shown. Do the same to the other end of the ear but not to the central part. The ear is done for now. Don't forget you need to make another one of these.

8 Put your thumb on the rabbit's future face, and flatten it a bit. Then, with the help of a stick of any sort, poke two holes into the upper part of the future head, at one o'clock and eleven o'clock. This is where the ears will go. Make sure the holes are deep enough to accommodate about a quarter of an ear.

9 Put the ears in the holes, as shown, and gently squeeze the surrounding head to keep them firmly in place. You can also use a clay shaper to smooth the seam from the back of the ear. Bear in mind that because we are not using any armature at this point, it is quite natural for the ears to flap in the wind while you work on the rest of the rabbit. Just be careful not to rock their foundation (where they are fastened to the head).

10 Fold one of the ears in two and a little to the side, without covering the lower, inner yellow part. (Rabbit ears are quite revealing—this position implies a wink.)

11 Use a pin to draw the rabbit's face. Lightly trace the basic features where a more sophisticated face will soon smile.

12 Put the tip of the tapered-point clay shaper into the holes for eyes, and, with a rotating motion, widen the craters to make eye sockets.

13 Using the cup-round clay shaper, open the rabbit's mouth, as shown here.

14 Using purple polymer clay for the eyelids and glow-in-the-dark clay for the eyeballs, make the rabbit's eyes. Then put them into the eye sockets. The eyes are made exactly like those in the bird lesson. (See page 11 to review detailed eye making instructions.)

15 Make a small blue dome, or a hemisphere, to put in the center of the critter's face. This new protrusion will serve as a pedestal for the rabbit's nose.

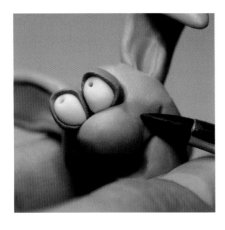

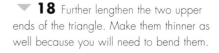

18 Further lengthen the two upper ends of the triangle. Make them thinner as well because you will need to bend them.

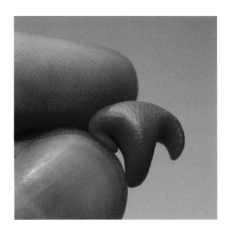

▲ **16** Put the blue dome in the center of the rabbit's face, right under his eyes. Then, using the tapered-point clay shaper, blend it into the whole.

▲ **17** After all this preparation, we're ready for the nose. Using pink polymer clay, make a triangle with three equal sides. You can use any other shade of polymer clay, but the goal is to achieve the effect that is a specialty of another imaginary character—Rudolf the Red-Nosed Reindeer. Squeeze the triangle as shown.

▲ **19** Bend the two ends down toward the bulk of the nose to make the nostrils.

▼ **20** While it is still warm, stick the nose to the rabbit's face.

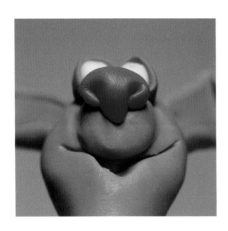

◀ **21** Next, we make the rabbit's cheeks. The technique is largely the same as that used previously for the bird. Here, however, we'll give more volume to the shape in the center. Make the two ends pointy.

TIP

Stickiness of Clay

When you work on a piece of clay, it warms up and becomes stickier, from all the kneading and the temperature of your hands. The stickiness makes the bonds between the clay pieces stronger. Use that property to make a critter that breaks less. Don't wait too long before you attach add-on parts to the bulk of a critter, especially when you do not intend to blend the add-on shape with its surroundings using a clay shaper, like you did with the little dome a couple of steps ago.

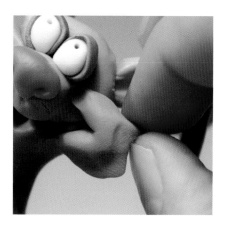

▲ **22** Curve the shape into a croissant, and attach it to the face. Place one of the sharp ends near the lower outer corner of the eye and the other no further than where the neck starts—unless, of course, you want the rabbit to have sagging cheeks.

▲ **23** Pinch the rabbit's cheeks between your index finger and thumb. (Just like one of these uncles who always say, "Look how much you've grown!")

▲ **24** Using that same index-finger-and-thumb hold, but in a perpendicular direction, pinch the cheeks some more, using the tip of your nail to create a sharper shape.

▲ **25** Repeat the same action again, further down the cheek.

▲ **26** Drawing in the clay with a needle or a pin makes the critter's features stand out. It also helps to highlight shapes. Stick the tip of the pin almost between the eyes, and draw a curved line toward the lower outer corner of the eye.

▲ **27** Draw the eyebrows. Make sure they are slanted like this— / \ —to give the critter a good-natured look.

◄ **28** Use the pin to make the hair. You need to be more energetic with the pin—stick it deeper and break the clay while drawing it out to create the effect of hair. It is more important to create the impression of small tufts than to focus on individual hairs.

30 Use the pin to separate the two teeth. Start from the lower end of the teeth, and press toward the upper lip. By using the upper lip for resistance, you not only create a better shape but also fasten the teeth more firmly.

31 Make a ball out of the yellow clay, and squash it into a disk. Stick the disk to the belly of the rabbit, and give the creature a belly button by using a pin. Ideally, the belly button should not be in the center of the circle but a little toward the lower part.

29 Create the teeth by sticking a longish piece of white polymer clay to the upper lip.

32 Now its time to create the feet. Round off all the sharp edges from a piece of blue clay, and, referring to the photo, hold the two ends and exert some pressure toward the middle.

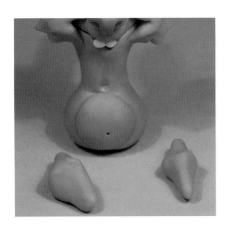

35 The two feet overlap, because this is a very modest rabbit. They are less likely to break off, as well, once you have baked the critter. You shouldn't always let the fragility of materials dictate the posture of your creations (for example, we ignored it while making the ears), but if functional limitation can be reconciled with artistic goals, as it can be in this case, why not?

33 This is how big the feet are in proportion to the body. In addition to having long ears, rabbits are supposed to have big feet, because they run fast. So there is no real danger of overdoing the feet—make them as large as you want. The proportion shown in the picture is only a recommendation.

34 Attach the feet to the bottom of the critter. Make sure they are perpendicular to the body so that the rabbit will be well balanced.

36 The hands are made using a basic technique you are already familiar with from making the bird's toes. Make the fingers from the same little shapes that have one pointy end and one round end. Then make the arm the same way, the only difference being that it is longer. The majority of the critters in this book will have four fingers, which is a popular convention when it comes to cartoon characters. Typically, the index finger here should be slightly bigger than the middle finger and the pinkie, and the thumb should be slightly chubbier.

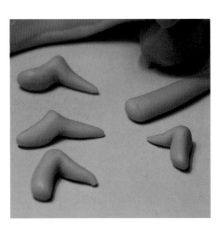

37 Bend a bunny finger between your index finger and thumb to create a joint, as shown. Repeat for all the fingers and the arm itself, too.

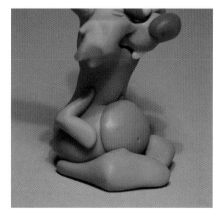

38 The arm and hands are added bit by bit to the body of the critter. First, attach the arm on the side, where the neck ends and the torso starts.

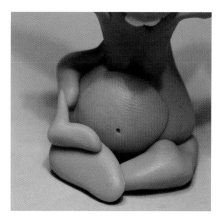

39 Attach the pinkie firmly, so that the pointy end is attached to the bottom of the arm and the thick end is on the hand.

40 In the same way, proceed with the next finger, making sure that it is firmly attached and that it doesn't entirely cover the previous one.

41 The base of the thumb makes a right angle with the other fingers and also covers the spots where they are attached to the arm. Use a clay shaper to smooth the surface and make all the joints firmer. Add the opposite arm.

42 Adding an Easter egg is the easiest way to transform an ordinary rabbit into an Easter Bunny. Roll out a small egg of red polymer clay. Stick it firmly to the body where the arm that is supposed to hold it ends. We will put the egg first and then add the fingers around it.

43 Using the same steps as for the other hand, add the fingers one by one. The only difference this time is that they have to be firmly wrapped around the egg without covering too much of it.

44 To make the tail, stick a ball of blue clay to the bottom of the Easter Bunny. This appendage should also counter any backward motion it might be inclined to make.

45 The Easter Bunny is nearly finished. To add a last touch of charm, use the safety pin to draw stitches (long lines crossed with shorter ones) along all the central axis of the critter. That way the Easter Bunny will look like a toy. This is also a good time to draw the individual toes on the bunny's foot. Finally, draw a crack on the egg—an egg that is about to hatch is much more exciting.

Bake the rabbit following the clay manufacturer's instructions, and let it cool. For more tips on baking, see page 7.

TIP

Fingerprints—or Why You Should NOT Try to Get Rid of Them

According to some people, fingerprints should be removed. However, fingerprints offer many positive things. First, most creatures have a certain sort of texture to their surfaces—unless, of course, we are talking about an alien, a frog, or a porcelain vase. The fingerprints that you leave fulfill that function of creating a texture, which produces a more natural look. A fantasy character does not need to look real, but it does need to look natural to a certain degree to be believable.

Second, you have to come very close to a creature to see the fingerprints. (But is this not the case with most things—the closer you come, the more you see the imperfections? It's a natural phenomenon.)

Last, but not least, your fingerprint is your signature that can never be forged. By leaving your fingerprints, you give the creatures identity in both the figurative and the literal sense.

Variation Ideas
Easter Bunny with a Basket, Easter Bunny with a Frying Pan

Easter Bunnies are, by definition, cute and must have an egg in their possession to distinguish them from ordinary rabbits. Play with these two general truths to produce the maximum humorous effect. The Easter Bunny with a basket pictured at right has gathered a few small eggs in his basket. The bunny in the picture at right didn't quite get the idea and thought he could still be an Easter Bunny if he made fried eggs. Also, if you look closely, all rules of symmetry are disobeyed, resulting in a rabbit that looks more deranged than cute.

 **1** To make a frying pan, start with a mushroomlike shape.

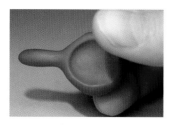

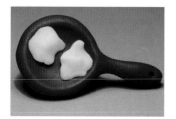

2 Press in the center of the thicker part with your thumb, while holding the other side with your index finger. Define the round inner edge of the frying pan with your fingernail. Rotate the pan, repeating the same action.

3 Add two white amoebas.

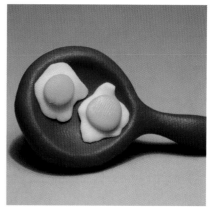

4 Add the yolk—two squished balls of yellow clay. Yummy! Note that the bunnies' legs are apart this time, so that they can serve as a support for the pan. The hands are, as usual, built around the item that the rabbit is holding.

The Three Easter Bunnies

Or How to Make a Humanlike Creature

This is the first humanlike creature we will make. Because we are not using any armature, we will try to optimize the properties that polymer clay has to offer and make a critter as unbreakable as possible— a creature with a bulky body firmly attached to the head and small arms and legs, close to the body. We will, therefore, put a particular emphasis on making the face and creating a whimsical facial expression to make it interesting.

MATERIALS

½ sheet flesh or beige clay
(we used Super Sculpey)
⅛ block glow-in-the-dark clay
⅛ block dark blue clay
⅛ block brown clay
⅛ block light blue clay
⅛ block pink clay
⅛ block green clay
⅛ block yellow clay
⅛ block orange clay
⅛ block purple clay
Pen spring

TOOLS

Small tapered-point clay shaper
Small cup-round clay shaper
Needle or safety pin

▼ **1** Start with the same "8" shape we used for the Easter Bunny, obtained by rolling a ball of clay between your index finger and thumb. We used Super Sculpey because of the flesh, or beige, color it offers.

 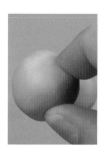

◀ **2** Most of the humanlike characters in this book will be "nose-centric." That means that to make a face we start with the nose, which serves as a reference point for making the rest of the facial elements. The nose in this project is a shape that is drawn from the bulk of the critter and not an add-on. Using the good old index-finger-and-thumb grip, hold the upper part of the future head, as shown.

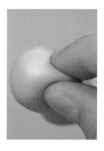 

◀ **4** Squeeze again in a direction perpendicular to the axis of the nose. This time, make sure your fingertips are not too close to each other, because the objective is to limit only the length of the nose.

▲ **3** Squeeze until your fingertips almost touch. The distance between your fingertips at the end of this squeeze will determine how wide the nose will be.

◀ **5** This is what the aspiring nose should look like. You can clearly see the marks your fingers left on the head. At this point you have a protrusion of sorts that can hardly be called a nose—something we'll take care of during the next steps. For now you just need to decide whether this is the general size desired. If it is, go on. If not, redo the same vertical and horizontal squeezes, in that order, "on top" of the old ones.

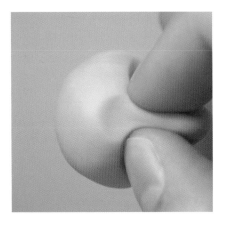

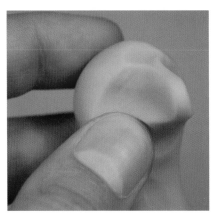

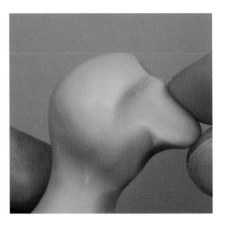

6 Although this step looks similar to the first one, it has a very different function—it smoothes the edges formed by the length-limiting squeeze and thus narrows the upper part of the olfactory organ so that it can blend seamlessly into the face. Your fingertips should be slightly parted at the lower end to avoid overthinning the whole nose.

7 The approach to the lower edges formed by the horizontal squeeze is quite different—we will use these to make the nostrils. Push carefully inward with your thumb (toward the brains of the critter, provided he has any) to define the nostril. Do this to the other nostril, too.

8 Gently put your fingers on top of the nose, as shown. After all this squeezing and pinching the nose has gotten quite thin, so to give it back some volume, you need to exercise pressure in a direction perpendicular (not opposite) to that of the squeeze.

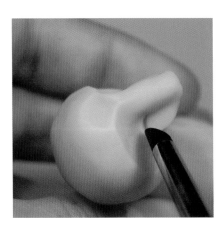

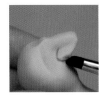

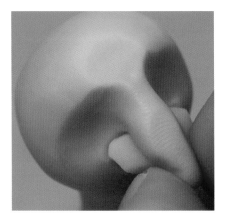

9 Using the tip of the cup-round clay shaper, accentuate the nostrils, as shown in these three pictures. Skipping from the nostril to the nose itself and back does not reflect a lack of consistency. Ideally, you would think that if you are working on a part of the critter, you should not move on before you are done with it. That linear approach, however, is not always the best strategy; as you concentrate on a certain area, chances are that you accidentally alter another one that you had considered finished. It makes a lot of sense to go back every now and then and see whether things are still the way you intended them to be.

10 And now—back to the nose. Pinch it once more, to make sure that the nostrils and the tip of the nose are nicely separated.

11 Nostrils are generally perceived to be two holes in the nose. We have been ignoring that crucial aspect of things quite successfully so far, but now is the time to conform to general truths. Using the tapered-point clay shaper, push in the direction of the outer shape to make a hole. Push until you see the clay on the outside of the nostril move a little bit. Be careful not to pierce the nostril.

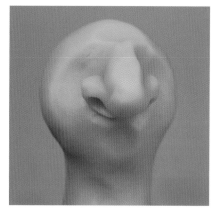

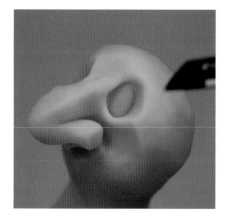

12 This is what the nose should roughly look like. Two elements should be present: slightly flared nostrils and, between them, the bulk of the nose. Finally, we can move on to the rest of the face.

14 Make an eye by wrapping a small ball of glow-in-the-dark clay in a flat piece of body-colored clay. You now have an eyeball with an eyelid.

13 Use the cup-round clay shaper to make an eye socket. Where you put the eye socket will largely determine if the nose will seem longer or shorter. The recommended choice here is that you put the eyes somewhat close to the nostrils.

15 Place the eye in the eye socket. Do not push it all the way down, but, rather, leave a hollow space under the eyeball. Otherwise, you risk blending the eyeball too much into the flesh tone. Proceed in the same way with the other eye, or at least make an eye patch.

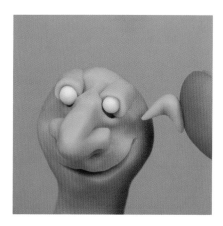

16 Using a needle, draw the mouth of the critter. Drive the needle deep into the clay. This step will be useful for opening the mouth to put teeth in later. Each end of the mouth should be pointing upward. To make the corners of the mouth—an integral part of some smiley faces—we will use a shape rather than just drawing in the clay. Make a small clay worm, and bend it in the middle, as shown. The benefit of such a mouth corner is that it creates the impression of a cheek.

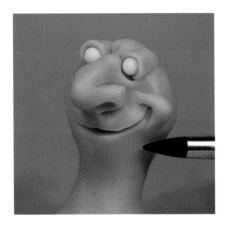

◀ **18** This is an additional upper lip. Because putting your little finger in the critter's mouth has probably curved the original upper lip (nobody's fingernails are entirely flat), you will need to make this addition.

▲ **17** Using a tapered-point clay shaper, blend the cheek into the face. Hold the creature from the back, and use your pinkie to open the mouth. Your fingernail should be under the upper lip.

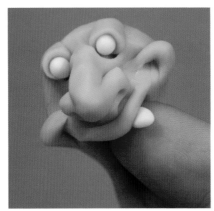

◀ **19** Put the upper lip in place, and smooth it at the ends. Make sure that the lip you are adding is slightly shorter than the distance from cheek to cheek so that you don't have to alter the mouth corners.

To start adding the teeth, roll a small, irregular shape of glow-in-the-dark polymer clay, and squish it flat. Then put it on your fingertip, and, as shown, attach it to the upper lip. Proceed similarly with the other teeth. How many teeth you put in the creature's mouth is entirely up to you. If you want the critter to seem anatomically correct, make sure that the central two teeth are more or less under the nose.

▶ **20** Now push the whole of the head back to the body to close the mouth.

Notice the wrinkles that form under the cheeks. Smooth them away using the tapered-point clay shaper. Because a natural way of holding the creature while working on it is to hold it by the neck, the wrinkles may disappear as you progress, simply because you touch them frequently.

▼ **22** Using the cup-round clay shaper, repair any damage to the corners of the smiling mouth caused by the opening and closing procedures.

▶ **21** Using the cup-round clay shaper, draw bags under the critter's eyes, as shown. Every shape you draw using the clay shapers can later be sharpened with the needle—just repeat the line with the tip of the needle right before you bake the critter. This move is particularly rewarding when you work with flesh-colored clays, because drawing in them creates soft details with a low contrast.

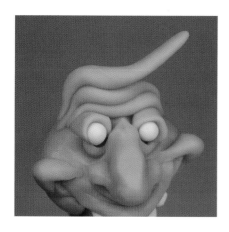

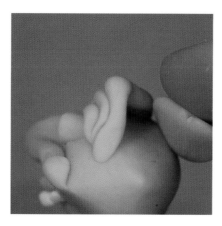

24 Add a piece of clay behind the forehead to give the head some more volume. The critter's hair and hat will later cover this part of the head.

▲ **23** This step is dedicated to making a wrinkled forehead. Every wrinkle is achieved by putting one worm of clay on top of another. Here we have used just three layers, but the principle is the same even when making a highbrow creature. The ends of the clay worms need to be blended so that the forehead does not look too fragmented. Use a clay shaper to smooth all edges.

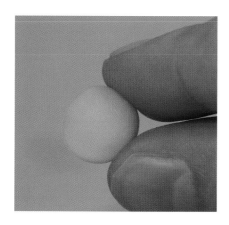

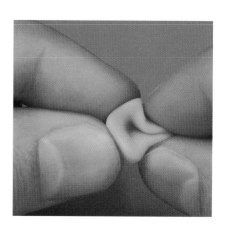

▲ **25** To make the ears, start with a disk of clay, a ball squished flat between your index finger and thumb.

▲ **26** Fold one end of the disk, as shown.

▲ **27** While still holding the shape you created, exert some pressure in the opposite direction. What we have now is not quite anatomically correct, but we are after the impression of an ear, not a clinical example of one. An ear is a complicated shape. Making real ears is difficult. Making fantasy ears can, in some sense, be even harder because we don't know what they look like. Therefore, an approximation will not only do—it is an excellent solution.

▶ **28** Attach the ear to the head, and smooth the seam with a clay shaper. You can also make two holes and plant the ears there, like we did in the Easter Bunny project.

Referring to the photograph, roll out a shape with a lot of volume that tapers off suddenly toward both ends. This shape will serve as a chin.

▲ **29** Attach the chin so that it touches the teeth. Then, using the cup-round clay shaper, give the creature dimples, as shown. Dimples, just like freckles, make critters look cute.

"Open" the eyes, and put two holes in the glow-in-the-dark eyeballs using a needle.

▲ **30** Now, we make the critter's eyebrows. Make two clay worms out of the flesh or beige clay and two smaller ones out of dark blue clay. Put them on top of the eyelids as shown, with the blue ones placed last.

▼ **33** We added two more pieces of brown clay to make a hairstyle of some sort. Most of the hair will go under the hat, but you should explore what a critter would look like without a hat as well. The fact that you are going for a jester should not discourage you from playing with all the opportunities your critter presents. If it looks to you that he is more fit to be a school teacher than a joker, give him a tie and a book instead of following the rest of the instructions. Abandoning your initial goal does not show a lack of conviction. On the contrary, it allows you to help a critter realize its true potential. You have made a face, and it is that face that will suggest what type of creature you have made. The clothes and items he holds are only accessories.

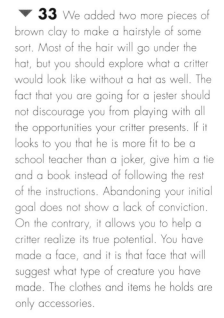

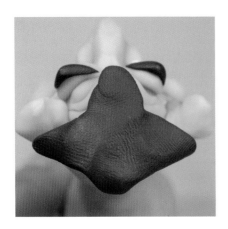

▲ **31** It is time to give your bald critter some hair. Referring to the photo, use brown clay to make a shape with three jutting points.

▲ **32** Wrap the brown-clay hair around the oval of the head.

35 Look closely at the picture—what finally makes the ear are two traces of the cup-round clay shaper, the upper one of them slightly larger than the lower one.

▲ **34** This brings us to a crucial step that involves more meditation than action. Here is the face we have made so far. We decided that it was a jester's face, after all, so we went on to squish his ears flat, because they seemed to have too much edge.

◀ **36** The hat consists of three cones of well-contrasting colors. On top of each cone, attach a small ball of orange polymer clay. Then put the bases of the three cones together, with their tips apart. Stick the whole hat firmly on top of the hair. As you can see, no sign of hairstyle is visible anymore.

This is also the moment when we add a small clay worm as a lower lip, blending its two ends into the chin using a clay shaper.

▶ **37** No, these are not the Olympic rings. This is how you make a multicolored shirt for the jester. Stick a couple of balls of different colors of clay to each other, as shown. Then squeeze them between your fingers to flatten them into an irregularly shaped patchwork.

▶ **38** Wrap the patchwork around the jester's body, using the excess clay to make the base flat. To make legs, create two conic pieces of clay and attach them to the bottom of the figure. Then, holding the dressed body, firmly press the critter against your work surface to make sure that his bottom and legs are in the same plane and that the jester will not tip over.

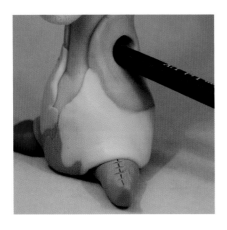

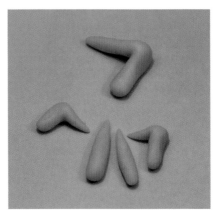

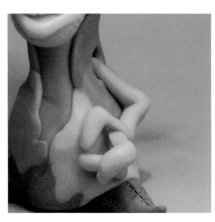

▲ **39** It is now time to make some preparation for the arms. Using the handle of the clay shaper, make a hole at the height of the shoulder. This is where you will put the arm in step 41.

▲ **40** The arms are made, as in the Easter Bunny project, out of tiny clay worms bent in the middle. The arm itself is bigger than the fingers; otherwise, the principle is largely the same.

▲ **41** Firmly attach the elements of the arm to the body in their usual order. First the arm, then the fingers, one by one and on top of each other—the little finger, the middle finger, the index finger, and, finally, the thumb, perpendicular to the fingers. Note that this time the whole pinkie and the whole thumb end up attached to the body and not to the hand.

◀ **43** Place a small ball of a green clay on the end of the spring. Trace a smiley face using a needle.

▲ **42** And now comes the most exciting part—when we realize that the process of creation also involves destruction. Find an old pen. (We used a new one assuming the sacrifice was worth it.) Take out the spring, but do not dispose of the rest of the pen yet. Pull both ends of the spring apart until it stays that way. This new length of the spring should be roughly equal to the height of the critter. Then make a small cube out of blue polymer clay, stick the spring in the center of the cube, and push on all four sides simultaneously to fasten it firmly in place. You guessed right—this will be a jack-in-the-box.

◀ **44** Using the principles you have been mastering so far, make a small face. Remember that a jack-in-the-box is a toy, so perfection is the last thing we are aiming for. On the contrary, the more naïve and simple the face is, the better. Make sure to give it a big grin and a shiny nose.

▶ **45** Attach the box to the critter's body so that its bottom is in the same plane as the bottom of the critter and his feet. Have one side adjacent to the foot and another to the critter's body. The arm that will be holding the toy should be somewhere close, too. We will put the fingers around the box, trying to give them maximum contact surface with the box itself, the critter's tummy, and the foot.

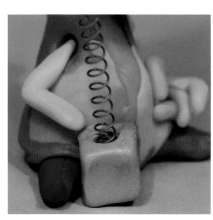

46 This might look like the step when the jester comes to life and takes over, but it is still you in charge. Squish two balls of clay into irregular disks, and cover the shoulder holes thus making short sleeves. Then make small, multicolored balls, and stick them on the jester's shirt wherever you think buttons are needed. The very operation of "sticking" them should be enough to flatten them. Using a needle, draw in the clay to separate the colors of the shirt with stitches and seams, and make four holes on each button. Finally, trace the edges of the box, and, using the tubular pieces of pen that you did not throw away, press on the visible corners of the box to make small circles.

47 After the long penultimate step, as a reward, comes an optional final step. Use the tip of the needle make as many small holes as close to each other as possible on the jester's face to create the impression of an unshaven critter. Five o'clock shadows are not a must, but if you choose to add this feature, be careful not to cover certain areas, such as the critter's lips.

TIP

Considering Facial Proportions

When creating cartoonish characters, it always helps to keep some idea of what a serious character looks like. Here are some rules you might find helpful to learn, so that you can do a better job at breaking them:

- The distance between two eyes is the length of an eye.
- The ears and the nose are of roughly equal length and are at the same level.
- The distance from the chin to the nose is equal to the length of the nose, which is equal to the distance from the nose to the hairline.

48 Here is the finished creature. Notice that the face of the jack-in-the-box and that of its owner are close to each other, so that when you look at the jester your attention is not divided between two distinct points of interest. When the faces are close to each other it is "easier" to look at the figurine.

Bake the character following the clay manufacturer's instructions, and let it cool. For more tips on baking, see page 7.

This project follows the basic rules we covered in learning how to make a jester with a jack-in-the-box. Although Hans is also a humanlike character, the very fact that he is made of a color other than flesh tone already is enough to suggest that he is not a human being. We explore this aspect of his personality somewhat further by giving him a tail and...well, you will find out very soon. The focus is on making a creature with less detail that nonetheless has a lot of character.

1 block orange clay

¹/₈ block glow-in-the-dark clay

¹/₄ block black clay

¹/₄ block pink clay

Small cup-round clay shaper

Small tapered-point clay shaper

Needle or safety pin

▼ **1** Start with a shape from the orange polymer clay that looks like a flat potato.

▼ **2** Here again we will use the principle of "nose-centricity" as a guiding rule. Gently squeeze in the upper part of the flat potato. Here the objective is to make a nose that does not protrude too much from the face of the critter. You can see in the picture the marks your fingertips are supposed to leave on the clay. The small ridge between the two dents will serve as a nose...

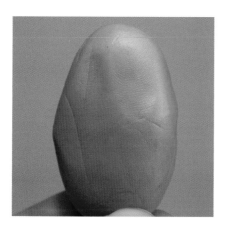

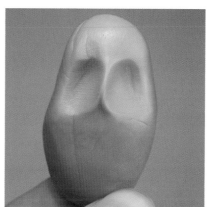

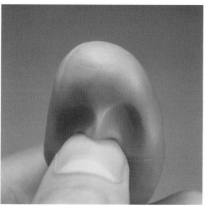

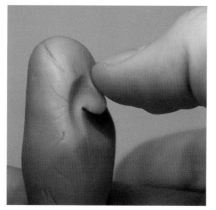

▲ **3** ...with some further modifications that we will now make. Push with your thumb so that your nail cuts the ridge where it is at its highest.

▲ **4** Push down on the nose, as shown.

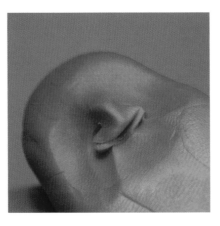

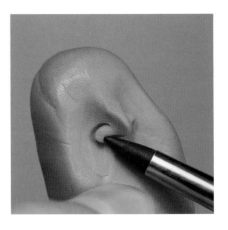

▲ **5** Use the cup-round clay shaper, and, with a rotating motion, draw out the nostril curve from the outside. Because we are using colored polymer clay (rather than flesh tone), the shapes appear better defined so you do not have to repeat the line with the needle as we did in the previous project.

▲ **6** In this photograph, you can see the mark the clay shaper left on the face while forming the nostril shape. Note that the clay shaper intervention goes all the way under the nose of the critter.

▲ **7** Use the tapered-point clay shaper to put the holes in the nostrils. The goal again is to make nostrils that are slightly flared, which imparts a more intense facial expression.

◀ ▼ **9** Repeat the same exercise, close to the first marks, and a third time, twice as high. The two sets of moons will serve as bags under the eyes of the critter. You do not need to exert too much pressure; just make sure that the tip of the clay shaper leaves distinct marks.

▲ **8** Using the cup-round clay shaper, put two "moons," or arches, on both sides of the nose.

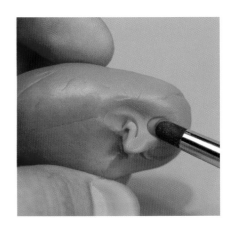

▲ 10 Use the clay shaper's handle to poke two holes above the uppermost moons to make eye sockets.

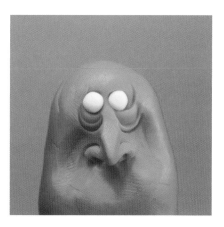

▲ 11 Roll two balls of glow-in-the-dark polymer clay, and insert them into the eye sockets.

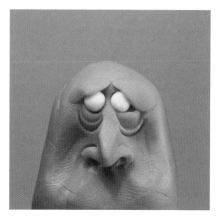

▲ 12 Use two flat pieces of clay to cover the eyes, as shown. Because this critter will be holding a heart, we want it to look a little sentimental, so the eyelids should obey the "/ \" rule.

▲ 13 Now it is time for some needlework. Poke two holes in the eyes, and draw the smile of the critter.

▲ 14 Make a short, chubby clay worm, bend it in the middle, and use it to cover the mouth corner. Smooth the wrinkles between the critter's eyes with the clay shaper—we do not want a creature that is knitting its eyebrows.

▲ 15 Using the cup-round clay shaper, put dimples in the critter's cheeks. You can also use the needle for a deeper effect.

▲ **16** Using the tapered-point clay shaper, erase any traces of the mouth drawing that are still visible under the cheeks. Then widen the mouth. We will need to add teeth soon.

Take this opportunity to draw "the wrinkles of laughter," converging in the lower outer corner of the eyes, as well as a set of eyebrows.

▲ **17** Put a tiny strip of glow-in-the-dark polymer clay into the mouth. You don't have to fill the whole mouth.

▲ **18** Use the needle to separate the teeth from one another. Stick the needle close to the lower lip without touching it, and draw it toward the upper lip.

▼ **21** Bend the lower end of the ear slightly forward to form the ear lobe. We will have only one pointy end on the ears.

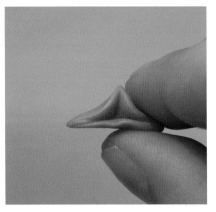

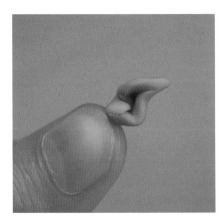

▲ **19** To make an ear, use a flat, round piece of clay. Fold or pinch one end of it, as shown.

▲ **20** Fold the other end in exactly the same manner. You should achieve a triangular shape with one long and two equal sides.

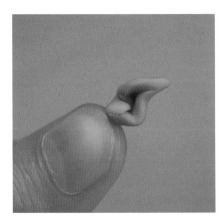

▶ **22** Attach the ears firmly to the head.

▲ **23** Now for the feet. Referring to the photographs, make a shape with volume in the center, tapering off toward the two ends. Make two of them.

◀ **24** Turn the critter upside down, and attach the feet to its bottom. This is the time to draw his torso, and his belly button in particular. (Although the critter's chest will soon be covered with an enormous bow tie, it is a good idea to see what he would have looked like had you decided to put him in a bathing suit.)

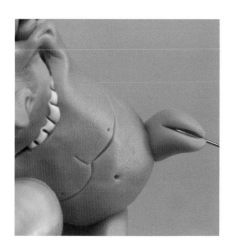

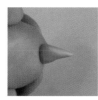

◀ **26** Turn the critter around. It is time to give him a tail. Using the clay shaper's handle, make a hole in the body. Then insert a piece of clay so that half of it is in the critter and the other half, a roughly conical shape, sticks out. The tail needs to be firmly attached to the body. (This peg-and-hole technique is the same one used to fasten the Easter Bunny's ears.)

◀ **27** Make an isosceles triangle (all sides of equal length), and add it to the tail, as shown. The peculiarity of this triangle is that its sides are not made of straight lines but slightly curved ones. (It is a cliché that "straight lines do not exist in nature." Of course, the creatures we make here all exist in nature, so avoiding straight lines is a must. This is why we rarely use a cutter. All you need to do to make the perfect triangle, for our purposes, is to use your fingers.)

▲ **25** Transform the feet into hooves. Simply divide the foot in two using the needle, as shown.

▲ **28** This is an optional step for those of us who are concerned with fragility. You can stick the tail against the critter's back, thus avoiding any risk of it breaking off.

▶ **29** It's dress-up time! Make a bow tie out of two black triangles by attaching them one at a time to the critter's chest. A tie is usually made of fabric, making our "avoid straight lines" argument from two steps ago particularly valid.

▲ **30** This is the good old clay worm, bent in the middle, that we like to call a finger, or, if it comes in a bigger size, an arm. Make three small worms and one big worm. Repeat. Do not assemble the hands yet—we will add them bit-by-bit to the bulk of the critter later.

31 Now we'll start making the thing the critter will be holding—a heart. A heart starts with a piece of pink polymer clay squished almost flat.

32 Making a heart shape is somewhat self-explanatory, but bear in mind that you need to preserve its volume. The heart should not be too flat, because we will need to attach it to the body by its depth dimension. The bulkier the heart is, the greater contact surface we will have and the stronger the bond will be.

33 This is roughly what the finished heart should look like. Notice once again that we avoided sharp edges. It looks more like an inflatable heart and not like a cookie-cutter heart cut from a uniformly thick sheet of clay. The secret is to use your fingers as much as you can.

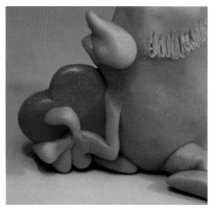

34 Attach the heart to the body, maximizing the contact surface. The pointy end of the heart is almost wedged between the leg and the body of the critter. You can see in the picture some of the fingers you previously made and left lying around. Turn the critter around to see how they ended up there.

35 The arm is attached to the body and the heart at the same time, obeying the principle, "united we stand, divided we fall." The lower arm, in similar fashion, makes contact with the foot, and the fingers are either attached to the back of the heart or wrapped around it from underneath, which is why you could see them from the front. Use a clay shaper to make all joints seamless, as usual.

Use the needle to draw some hairs on the back of the head, to avoid the monotonous uniform mass of orange polymer clay that was there before.

36 To make the free hand, start with the arm and then add the fingers one by one, as shown. First comes the little finger, with the middle and index fingers on top of it. The thumb comes last, attached perpendicularly to the other fingers. The fingers have to end up somewhere close to the lower-left corner of the bow tie—you will see why shortly.

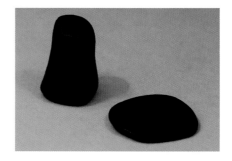

37 Make the two elements of the hat: a disk of black clay and a cylinder, which is slightly narrower toward one end.

38 Put the disk on the critter's head. Then stick the narrow end of the cylinder on top of it. Make sure to press hard each time to form a strong bond. Place two small conical shapes on both sides of the head to give the critter horns. Tilt them around a little bit for a comical effect.

39 The critter, whom we decided to name Hans, is almost finished. Notice that the index finger and thumb of his left hand are touching his bow tie. To achieve that effect you might have to pull gently on the lower-left corner of the tie, toward the fingers, and then press the fingers together around it. It looks like you made a critter who is aware of his own existence!

TIP

What *Should* a Clay Critter Hold?

As we have discussed, the first thing that defines the personality of a fantasy character is his face. This suggests that if a critter has an evil face, for example, we should probably put an ax in his hands, so that his occupation would be in tune with his natural inclination. However, such unison, although apparently logical, should not necessarily be a goal. More interesting results are gained when a contrast between a creature's looks and his business exists—if you put a cute bird in a villain's hand, you are likely to raise some eyebrows, but what you will achieve is a humorous effect. People will ask themselves, "What on earth is going on here?" and that is the key to an intriguing critter.

Algebra and Ethics

If you want to alter a portion of a creature you have made, it is always easier to add more clay than to take some out. The very process of taking out a piece often involves messing up its surrounding elements; try pushing the undesirable shape in, compressing it into the bulk of the critter instead. Then you can add more clay to remake the compressed part. To sum up, addition is good, subtraction bad.

Symmetry

The face of a critter does not need to be symmetric, so don't waste any time trying to make the left eye more like the right one. You can easily confirm that this is true on yourself with the mirror-and-picture test. Put a mirror along the central axis of a picture of yourself, and you will find that the picture half and its mirror counterpart form a face that is not quite yours. More generally this is true for the body of the critter as well.

40 At this final stage we have a huge black hole in the middle of the critter—his bow tie. The more conservative among you will argue that this is sheer elegance, but what would happen if we just made a lot of minute glow-in-the-dark balls and scattered them around the two black triangles?

Finally, draw a stitch in the middle of the heart, a positive message—that broken hearts can be mended—to send your audience. Audience is correct—no critter should be ever locked up in a cupboard.

Bake the critter following the clay manufacturer's instructions, and let it cool. For more tips, see the baking section in the beginning of this book.

You are about to make a fire-breathing dragon. We won't go so far as to show you how to put the fire in it, but we'll use some wire to make it at least a little formidable. This is the first project where you will learn how to use armature to put polymer clay into whatever shape you want. Polymer clay, usually quite spineless, is pretty adamant on one point—it will not stand straight when you try to make a bow-legged elf with a beer belly. The mass of the torso would invariably crush the thin legs unless you use armature.

2 blocks red clay
¼ block glow-in-the-dark clay
¼ block orange clay
⅛ block light brown clay
39" (1 m) 0.7 mm copper wire
Tin foil

Wire cutters
Flat-nosed pliers
Needle or safety pin
Small tapered-point clay shaper
Small cup-round clay shaper
Small tube

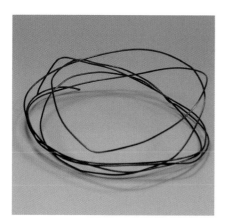

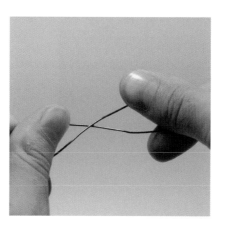

▲ **1** To make the armature, or the skeleton, of the dragon, we will use any wire that is flexible enough to be manipulated with bare hands and strong enough to support some clay on it. The wire used here is ordinary copper wire. You will need about 39" (1 m) of wire and a pair of wire cutters.

Always try to use one piece of wire for the whole skeleton to avoid having to make complicated joints between several short pieces of wire. The small scale we are working on permits the use of a single piece of wire, because the wire does not have to be long. Using one piece of wire for the armature is a little like drawing without lifting the pen from the sheet, so you have to carefully plan the sequence of steps, making sure that the two ends of the wire remain loose until you reach the tail of the critter.

▲ **2** We are using relatively soft wire for two reasons. First, it's easy to manipulate, and second, because we can double it by twisting two halves together. Fold the long wire bit in half and, holding it as shown, start twisting it together.

▲ **3** Leave a loop at the end—because you have to (there is nowhere to hold the wire if you want to continue), and because this is where the head will be.

This simple technique of doubling the wire turns out to be priceless when it comes to armature. It allows you to regulate how long or short the double-wire bit will be, and you can also control its hardness and flexibility. The tighter you twist it together, the shorter and stronger the doubled wire will be. Last, but not least, the clay will cling better to an armature that is not as smooth as a single wire would have been had we left it that way.

TIP

About Armature

You don't need to spend too much time perfecting an armature. Armature is only an approximation of a critter's skeleton, not a clinical reconstruction of a skeleton. It is perfectly fine to make a rough and asymmetrical structure, as long as the deviations are small enough to be corrected by the clay coat afterwards.

▲ **4** Referring to the photo, make two wings from the wire. Twist the two ends of the wire together below the wings.

▲ **5** Twist the wires of the two wings together to make a cross shape. Leave a little triangle in the middle, and twist the loose ends around each other for the last time.

▲ **6** Cut off the single loose ends of wire, and bend down the head loop and the wings, as shown. You will also need to get rid of the wing loops by squeezing them tightly together, perhaps with the help of a pair of flat-nosed pliers.

▲ **7** Wrap a piece of tin foil tightly around the central part of the cross to create more volume for the dragon's torso. Using tin foil for the core of the dragon allows us to create volume without creating a heavy mass; the finished critter will be lighter and you will save some clay. Of course, it is perfectly acceptable to use just clay to fill the empty stomach of the dragon if you wish. We are more concerned with appearance than essence—whatever you put inside a critter is acceptable, as long as the façade is pleasing to the eye. (You can leave a message to posterity on a small sheet of paper inside the dragon for when he finally breaks many years from now. It would be like putting a message in a flying opaque red bottle with scales and claws.)

▲ **8** Start covering the torso with clay of the color that you plan to use for the surface of the character.

▲ **9** Proceed in the same way for the limbs, until the whole thing starts looking like a bird of sorts. At this stage, the critter should have a round belly and a tapered tail.

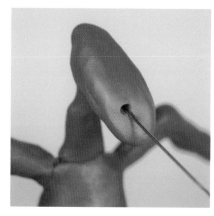

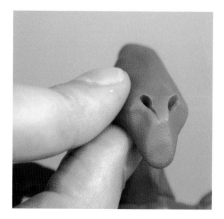

🔺 **10** Cover the head loop until the neck and the head start looking like an upside-down boot. Make sure that the "heel" stands out. We will next work on the head—it is much more rewarding to put wings and scales on a critter that already has a face.

🔺 **11** Using the needle, poke two nostrils in the upper-front part of the head. Rotate the needle a little to make the nostrils bigger.

🔻 **12** Gently squeeze the dragon's muzzle, as shown, right under the nostrils to give them a droplike shape. You should only exert pressure on the upper half of the head, almost on the very surface, rather than squeeze on the sides.

🔻 **13** Squeeze the dragon's snout between your index finger and thumb, as shown, to make it pointy. Then bend it down a little bit.

🔻 **14** Gently pull while squeezing on the sides of the head to make it a little wider. The underside of the head should be more or less flat.

▶ **15** Carefully push down the head while holding the neck with your thumb. This manipulation has two goals: first, it flattens the top side of the head a little bit, and second, it makes it easier to look at the dragon. If the dragon's head were to remain strictly perpendicular to the body an observer would have to rotate the critter (or their own head) to get a full impression of it—they wouldn't be able to see all the important elements of the critter in one glance. When the head is bent down you can see both his head and his body at the same time.

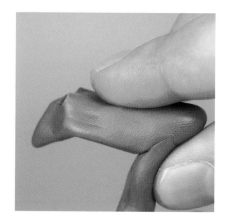

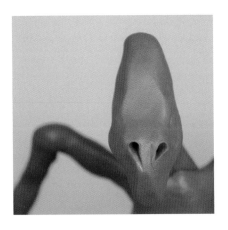

▲ **16** This is what the head looks like thus far.

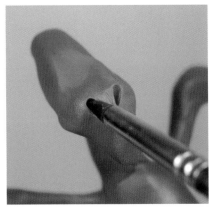

▲ **17** Stick the tapered-point clay shaper in the nostrils to make them a little wider and to make the outside of the nostril stand out.

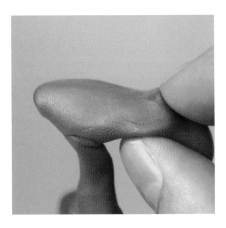

▲ **18** Put your finger, as shown, to flare the dragon's nostrils some more.

▼ **19** Use the clay shaper to put two holes in the upper part of the head. These holes will later serve as eye sockets.

We will now work on the wings. Working on different areas of a critter simultaneously can serve as a diversion and have a therapeutic effect—it is not unusual to get slightly bored when you concentrate on one area of a critter for a long time. As soon as you do not feel like dealing with a critter's nose anymore, feel free to turn to its feet, for instance. Remember that the purpose of all this is to have fun, and you should never let critter-making turn into another source of stress.

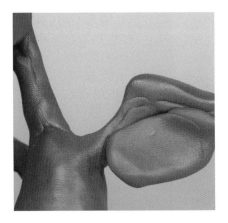

▲ **20** Attach a thick, flat piece of clay firmly to the wing's arm, as shown.

▼ **21** Start distributing the clay evenly until you fill up the whole space between the tip of the wing and the dragon's ribs. Be careful not to overthin the wing because there is no additional armature support that goes into it. An average thickness of about 1/10" (3 mm) is optimal.

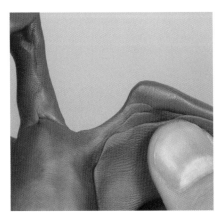

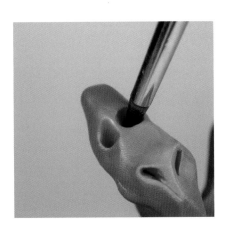

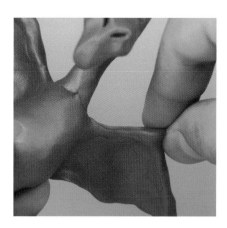

22 Pinch the wing elbow to make it pointier. This is the time to regulate the length of the lower and upper arms of the wing as well. Although there is armature on the inside, the clay that covers it does not need to follow the internal structure closely. Take advantage of this to make adjustments to the shape.

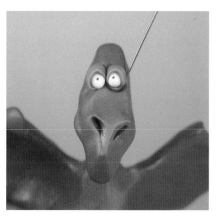

23 Wrap two pieces of glow-in-the-dark clay into orange clay, put them in the eye sockets, and poke two holes in them with the needle to create the dragon's eyes. Next, still using the needle, draw a curved line under each eye to accentuate it.

24 We will next make the lower jaw of the dragon. Start with a flat ellipse, then curve up the sides and form prongs, creating a shape like the one in the picture. Squeeze the two prongs so that they are flat in a direction perpendicular to the rest of the jaw. These prongs will help attach the jaw more firmly to the head.

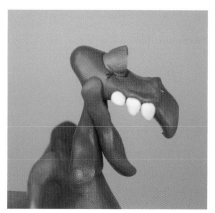

25 Attach the jaw to the dragon's head and to his neck. Now that the dragon's mouth is open, we should start putting teeth in it. Stick several irregularly shaped bits of glow-in-the-dark clay under the dragon's upper lip. The upper teeth should generally point downward, but to make them look jagged you can have them pointing in different directions.

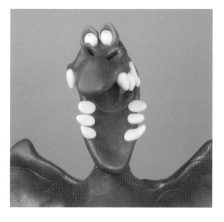

26 Gently push the jaws further apart and insert teeth on the lower jaw. This set of teeth should point outward. We will soon give the dragon a tongue, and if the teeth point upward now, it will be more difficult to insert the tongue into the mouth later.

49

27 The tongue is made from a flat piece of light orange clay. Squeeze on the sides to curl it up a little bit. Then put the tongue inside the mouth, and raise the lower jaw teeth to surround it. (See the sidebar on "Adding Clay in Difficult Access Areas," page 55.)

28 Give the dragon cheeks just like the ones we gave every other critter so far. Remember that the kind of cheeks we use are often mouth corners, too, so make sure to place them at the appropriate spot where the upper and the lower jaws join. Here is what the dragon looks like at this stage.

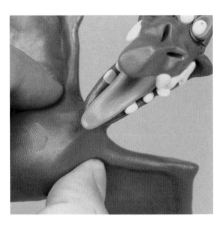

29 Squeeze the dragon's torso under the armpits so that the rounded belly protrudes even more.

30 With the tips of your fingers, pinch the lower part of the wings to create a few sharp points. A dragon's wing should look more like a bat's wing than a bird's wing. Two sharp points are enough to create that effect. The distances between these points should be slightly arched.

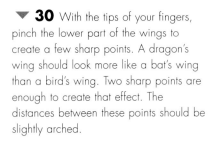

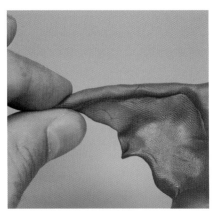

31 Sharpen the tip of the wings with your index finger and thumb, as shown.

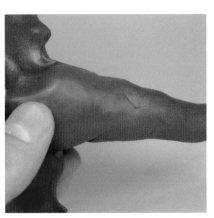

32 This is what the tapered tail of the dragon looks like at this stage. If it has thinned a lot because you have been holding the dragon by the tail while working on the other parts of his body, you may have to make it a little thicker by wrapping an extra sheet of clay around it and smoothing out the seams with the clay shaper.

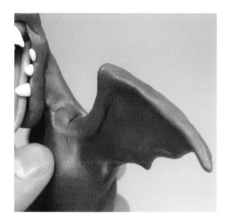

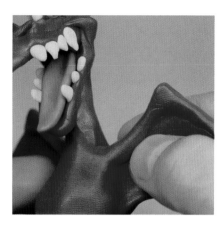

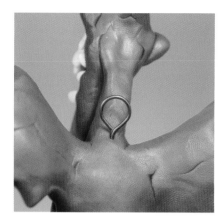

▲ **34** Push with your nail to define the part of the wing that has bones in it (what we have been referring to as the wing's arm). Slightly curve the skin surface of the wing.

▲ **33** By now you have probably realized that the dragon that we are making will indeed fly. In the next steps we will give him some mechanism by which he can be suspended in the air. There are many reasons for this choice. First of all, flying is an essential dragon characteristic. Second, a nonflying dragon would be more of a dinosaur, especially if you remove his wings (see the "Little Dinosaur" variation). And third, a winged dragon reduced to walking on the ground would look like a reptile and would have very little of the awe-inspiring quality that we are trying to achieve.

For all of these reasons, we will try to make the dragon look as if he is suspended in the air between two flaps of his powerful wings. Two concrete things you can do to achieve this—curve the tail slightly forward and to the side, and curve the lower arm of the wing.

▲ **35** Turn the critter around. To create the suspension mechanism, put a loop of wire in his back. To make this mechanism stronger, you should take the wire bit out before baking the critter. After baking the critter, fill the hole with extra strength glue and stick the wire back in. Don't forget to add the glue because the critter's life will literally hang on a thread.

An alternative way of tackling the suspension mechanism is to make the hanging mechanism from part of the armature cross. It is up to you to determine which option suits you best.

▲ **36** The next series of steps is dedicated to giving our dragon a nice glow-in-the-dark (or white) façade, which will consist of several plates, gradually increasing in size as you go down the belly. Start with the smallest, elliptical plate, and place it on the neck, under the lower jaw.

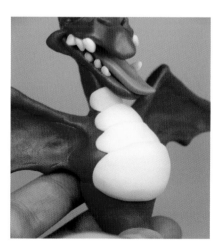

▲ **37** Gradually increase the size of every following plate, sticking them to the body in such a way that they slightly overlap each other.

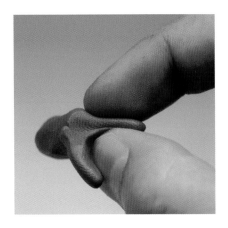

▲ **38** To make the legs, start with a chubby worm of clay. With your index finger and thumb, extract four toes, one at a time. (See the "Trutlio the Troll" lesson for more on extracted toes, pages 114-115)

▲ **39** The leg should look like a tree with a thick trunk and four bare branches.

▲ **40** Group three of the little branches together and place the last one (the thumb) opposite them. Slightly bend the tips of the branches of the tree structure inward.

▼ **41** Bend the whole leg in the middle to make the joint, and do not forget to make the knee pointy. Following the same procedures, make one more leg.

▼ **42** Attach the legs to the body, toward the lower part. They shouldn't be hanging loosely in the air, but, rather, pointing up or forward because the dragon makes a physical effort to stay in the air—he is not relaxed.

▼ **43** Use the same technique to make the arms. The only differences are that the dragon's hand has only two fingers, and the arm is a lot smaller than the leg. We are exploiting the familiar theme of the disproportionately small arms of the Tyrannosaurus Rex to produce humorous effect.

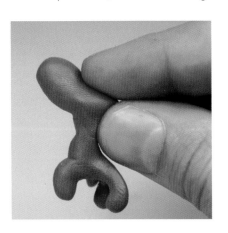

▶ **44** Attach the arms to the body at shoulder height and, using a clay shaper, blend them into the body. The upper part of the arm and the elbow should be attached to the torso.

To make the critter more expressive and to create the impression of movement, try not to have both arms or both legs in the exact same position.

▲ **45** Let's give the dragon some claws. To make a claw from orange clay, roll a short clay worm, and mold one end to a point. Stick the claws firmly on the toes. They should point inward.

▲ **46** In the same manner, proceed with the claws for the hands, only make them a little smaller. Use the needle give the dragon a bellybutton in the center of the biggest and lowest breastplate

▲ **47** By this time, you have probably noticed that it has become increasingly difficult to hold the dragon while you work without affecting another part of it. The problem is that we are not working with a critter who is simply sitting on a large, flat bottom.

Try using the hold in the picture, where your thumb is on the dragon's tail and your index finger (and possibly middle finger) is on his back, between the wings.

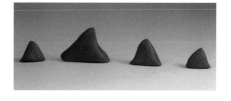

▲ **48** Could this be Nessie, the Loch Ness monster?

Relax—this is just a series of triangles (the kind whose sides are not straight lines) that need to go on the dragon's head and back. Make them in different sizes, and make sure that they have one thicker side—the one that will be attached to the dragon's body.

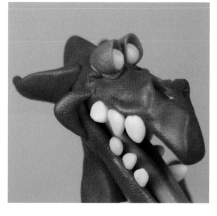

▲ **49** Put two of the larger triangles on the sides of the dragon's head, as shown, until it starts looking like the tail of an airplane. Slightly tip up the very end of these new "wings."

◀ **50** Turn to the back of the critter. On his tail, apply a series of index-and-thumb squeezes along the center of the back of the tail. This zigzag shape that we are introducing will echo the triangles that we will place along the spine.

▲ **51** Place a small triangle on the tip of the tail, which by now should be pointing up. Make sure to strengthen the bond by using a clay shaper and smudge the tip of the tail into the triangle.

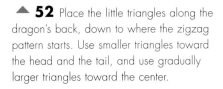

▲ 52 Place the little triangles along the dragon's back, down to where the zigzag pattern starts. Use smaller triangles toward the head and the tail, and use gradually larger triangles toward the center.

You have just completed the last stage of the sculpting process.

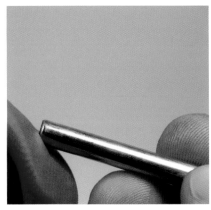

◄ 53 There still remain a few critical steps before we turn this creature into a real dragon. We need to give its skin some texture—a dragon without scales is no dragon.

To make the scales we will use any tool that would leave a circular imprint on the clay. We used a bit from a broken antenna but any other small tube shape, such as a straw, will do.

We will use only half of the tubular tool. Push half of the tube's cross section against the clay as shown to create a semicircle (experiment on a scrap piece of clay to practice). Repeat until you get a whole line of semicircles. Make another line of semicircles right above the first one with a lag of half a semicircle. Continue in this manner until you achieve a texture that looks like scales.

▲ 54 Apply the scale method to the dragon's body. Notice that you do not have to cover each square inch of the dragon with scales to make your point. Irregularly spaced patches of scales can be enough to create the desired effect.

▲ 55 Cover the wing's arm with scales, too, but leave the central part of the wing relatively smooth, so that you can draw in it with the needle to create the impression that the wing has some more sophisticated anatomy. Draw a few lines connecting the lower pointy tips with the wing's elbow.

▲ 56 When putting scales on the face, be particularly careful. If you put too much texture on the face the main facial features will not be as prominent as before. A few unfinished circles here and there will do.

▶ **57** Here is your finished charming monster. One last question remains—how can you bake it without flattening any part of it? You will need to make two cylinders of tin foil, so that the dragon can lie on his back with these cylinders going horizontally between his wings and the triangles in the middle of his back. These cylinders should be big enough to prevent the triangles or any other body part from touching the baking tray.

Bake the dragon following the clay manufacturer's instructions, and let it cool. For more tips on baking, see page 7.

TIP

Adding Clay in Difficult Access Areas

To put a piece of clay in an area where your fingers are too big to reach, use a clay shaper. Stick the bit of clay on the shaper's tip, insert it, push with the clay shaper to fasten it, and then withdraw the tool.

You can also use tools as a mediator when you are trying to get a piece of clay to stay on another piece of clay, but it stubbornly sticks to your finger instead. The fact that the bond between a tool and a bit of clay is much weaker than the one between two pieces of clay will work to your advantage.

The Order of Stickiness

Type of bond:	Strength of bond:
Clay to clay	Strong
Finger to clay	Medium
Tool to clay	Weak

Variation Idea
A Little Dinosaur

Dragons and dinosaurs are not all that different. By using the basic principles of this lesson and simplifying them, you are able to make this green little wingless character whose ancestors roamed the earth millions of years ago. It is nothing more than a small green wingless dragon baby.

Now that you have made a dragon, it would be wise, for security reasons, to make a knight. The knight we will be making in this project boasts some heavy armor, built almost entirely from metallic buttons, which, given the scale we are working in, turn out to make excellent shields, shoulder pads, and helmets. You will learn how to fasten the buttons to the clay so that their original function is completely forgotten and there is no clash between the medium of polymer clay and the expressive means of haute couture. The only uncovered bits of our otherwise well-protected warrior will be his face and one of his hands. We will reiterate the basic features of a funny face, introduced in earlier projects, and exploit them with yet another variation.

MATERIALS

½ block flesh or beige clay

⅛ block glow-in-the-dark clay

⅛ block black clay

½ block dark blue clay

¼ block blue clay

1 block silver clay

⅛ block red clay

⅛ block brown clay

6 metallic buttons—2 small, 3 medium, and 1 large

10" (25.4 cm) very thin wire

4" (10.2 cm) thin wire

4" (10.2 cm) of an old chain

1" (2.5 cm) of another old chain

1 feather

TOOLS

Small tapered-point clay shaper

Small cup-round clay shaper

Needle or safety pin

Wire cutters

Small tube

1 Start with an irregular shape, roughly similar to the one in the picture, about 1" (2.5 cm) high and slightly flat. As you knead, squeeze, and pinch the clay with your fingers, you will achieve rough shapes that we will develop further into facial features with the help of other tools. Consider the random shapes that a casual kneading of the clay generates not as something that need smoothing but, on the contrary, something to explore.

2 Put your thumb on the upper half of the future face, and flatten it a little. The trinity of eyes and nose will soon lie here, whereas the lower part will serve as the creature's chin and jaw and will host its mouth. Because we are making a knight, we can achieve comical effect either by exaggerating the stereotype of a tough, stocky fellow, without glasses or any other element that would betray his natural intelligence, or, alternatively, by making a tall, skinny chap with a fragile appearance who can hardly handle his armor. For this project we will opt for the first of these extremes; hence, a big lower jaw adds to the rugged stereotype.

3 Here is the flat mark that your thumb left on the future head of the knight. Rest assured this is not the last blow that he will receive in his career as a warrior.

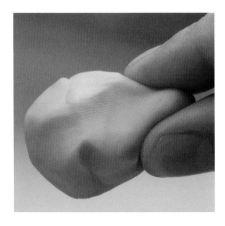 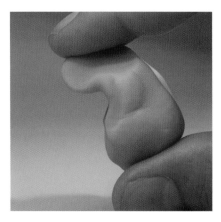 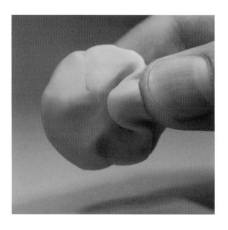

▲ **4** Squeeze the upper part of the head. As always, we are trying to extract the nose out of the mass of the head, and this and the next couple of steps are another possible approach to the extraction process.

▲ **5** Flip the head so that you can see its side (the flatness), and bend down the tip that was just between your index finger and thumb toward the plane of the face, as shown.

▲ **6** Push down on the nose toward the lower part of the head until the nose arrives almost in the center of the face where it rightfully belongs.

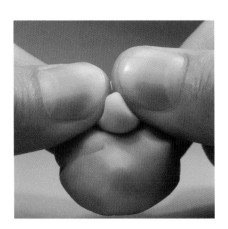 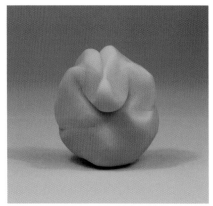 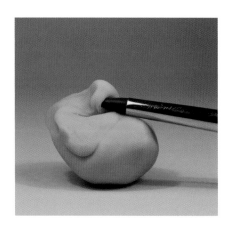

▲ **7** Try to make the protrusion of the nose more gradual. The push you made a moment ago generates two ridges that need smoothing. The ovals of your thumb tips are the ideal tool for this job.

▲ **8** You can see the marks your thumbs leave on both sides of the nose. The two bumps on the top are not a premeditated effect but a by-product of unsustainable nose extraction. Such side effects are desirable; the clay shapes itself as it pleases, and it is sometimes better to play along instead of trying to force it into a particular shape. Do not be alarmed if you do not get the two bumps, but don't try to make them—they are not essential.

▲ **9** Use the tapered-point clay shaper to open the nostrils. This exercise has two goals; first—to make the holes—and second—to push the clay into the bumps that are the exterior of the nostrils.

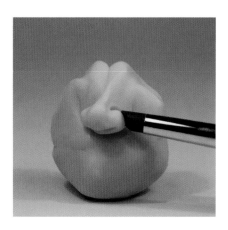

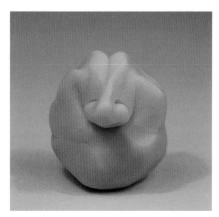

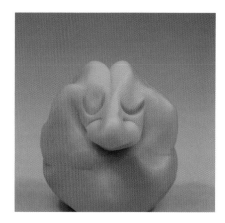

🔺 **10** Next, using the tip of the cup-round clay shaper, outline the outside of the nostrils.

🔺 **11** Here is what the finished nose looks like.

🔺 **12** Using the tip of the cup-round clay shaper, make two moons that gather water above the nostrils. We are preparing the ground for the eyes.

🔻 **13** Repeat the previous action, as shown, only this time press harder and slightly down with the clay shaper so that the tool leaves two shallow holes. The wrinkles of clay between the moons and the holes form the bags under the eyes of the creature.

🔻 **14** Turn the clay shaper around and poke two eye sockets into the head, slightly off center from the shallow holes from last step.

🔻 **15** Make two eyeballs small enough to fit into the eyeholes from glow-in-the-dark polymer clay. Then, poke two holes in them with a pin. Still using the pin, draw the mouth of the knight. Drive the pin deep into the clay; you will have to open the mouth shortly, and a superficial smile wouldn't be enough.

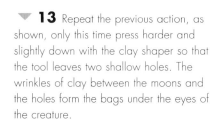

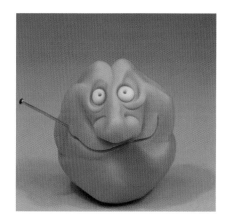

▶ **16** Make a mouth corner/cheek by rolling a small ball of clay between your index finger and thumb until it becomes slightly elongated, and then slightly bend it as shown.

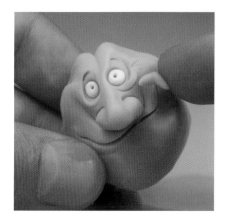

17 Using the same technique as in the previous step, make two slightly thicker clay worms, and put them above the eyes to form the foundation for the eyebrows.

Notice, in this picture, that one of the cheeks is bigger than the other. This asymmetry creates a more dynamic smile; the critter looks like he is smiling to one side, and, therefore, one of his cheeks is slightly more swollen.

Once again we are paying very little attention to absolute symmetry and relying on the differences between the right and the left side of the face to make it interesting. The only symmetry that we observe is in the fact that the critter has the same element on both sides of the face—an eye, a cheek, and an ear. But even this need not be true. If you are making a pirate, for example, and put an eye patch over one of his eyes, it will serve as a substitute to the counterpart of the real eye. What we are after is good composition rather than symmetry.

18 Open the mouth using the handle of a clay shaper.

19 Roll two thin black worms with pointy ends, and place them on the eyebrow foundations. Then close the mouth, leaving a small opening under the nose by pushing with your thumbs while holding the back of the head with your index and middle fingers. This opening-and-half-closing procedure is the easiest way to make a hollow for the mouth that looks believable. If you had left it at the previous step, the type of tools you used and how you dug the hole would be obvious. When you first open and then close, all such traces disappear, and it appears as if you somehow carved out the mouth cavity.

 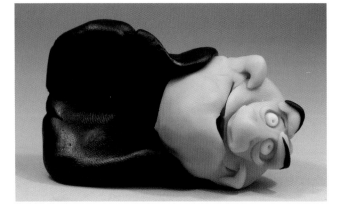

22 Roll a ball of blue polymer clay, and place it into the vessel formed by the dark blue cloak, adhering it to the critter's chin. This ball will be the knight's torso.

20 Using the dark blue clay, make a flat, thick trapezoid whose sides are irregular curves instead of straight lines. This shape will serve as the "backbone" of the knight's body, but it will look like a cloak on the outside.

21 Wrap the lower part of the head with the upper end of the cloak. Make sure that there is enough contact surface between the two parts to hold them together well. Our knight will simply not have a neck.

23 Next, make a slightly smaller ball of silver clay, squish it flat, and insert it under the blue ball. At the end of this step, you should have filled up the cloak entirely, as shown in the picture.

24 Buttons! Lots of buttons! You don't have to use the same type of buttons shown in the picture. They just need to be made out of some sort of metal. Beware of plastic buttons that have a metallic look, because they will not only melt when you bake the critters, but they may also emit poisonous fumes. In the picture you can see a general sample of the kinds of button that work. Generally, you need three sizes—one big button for the shield, three medium ones for the breastplate, the back plate, and the helmet, and two small ones for the shoulder pads.

25 Pick the coolest button you can find. Ideally it will be a button with an ornament on it or something that resembles a coat of arms. Cut 2" (5.1 cm) of very thin wire, and run the wire through the buttonhole. Twist the two ends around each other as close to the back of the button as you can.

26 Fold the wire in two, toward the button.

27 Place the wire in the center of the torso, and, holding the button, push it until it sinks in and the button sticks closely to the blue ball. The more tightly the wire is twisted the less wobbly it will be and the easier it will sink into the clay. When you bake the critter the hardened clay around the wire bit will hold the whole button in place.

28 With the tips of your index finger and thumb, give the squished silver ball edges, until it starts looking like a short cylinder. As you may have already guessed, this will be the lower part of the knight's garment.

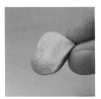

29 Let us jump to the head. Make three disks from the silver clay, and squish them flat. Create rectangles by making straight edges, as shown.

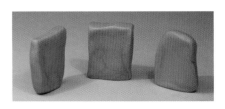

30 These rectangles are the building blocks of the helmet, other than the button. They need to have a little width.

31 Create a roof for the head. Because we did not bother to make ears, you should be able to easily stick two of the silver rectangles to the sides of the head. It's fine if they curve, following the oval of the head.

32 Stick the third rectangle horizontal to the back of the head.

33 Using the same wire technique as you did for the first button, fasten the "bumpiest" button you can find on top of the center of the head. Be careful not to distort the face too much while pressing the helmet button.

34 Make a flat shape from the silver polymer clay, as shown, to serve as a visor or neck guard. We use these terms in a very broad sense, because we are after only the impression of a visor or neck guard and not an accurate reproduction of a piece of medieval armor.

35 Add the visor/neck guard, covering the critter's chin and the upper part of the breastplate button.

36 Poke two holes at the desired height of the shoulders to host the arms.

37 Roll a silver cone, like the one shown.

38 Using the tapered-point clay shaper, make a hole in the base of the cone, and bend it into a right angle. The arm should look like a pipe at this stage.

40 Add a shoulder pad—one of the small buttons equipped with a piece of wire. The pad should form a 45-degree angle to the vertical axis of the critter and be attached in such a way that you can see the ornament directly as you are looking the critter in the face.

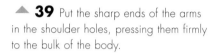

39 Put the sharp ends of the arms in the shoulder holes, pressing them firmly to the bulk of the body.

41 Turn the critter around. Because the shoulder button faces forward, the button's back is likely to be uncovered. Make a small silver bit of clay in the appropriate shape to cover the back of the button.

42 Here is what the back of the shoulder looks like. We have also added a medium-sized button to the back of the critter to make the uniform blue mass more interesting. Luckily, the button we found had an ornament that fits perfectly with our general theme.

43 What looks like a funny bowling ball is actually how you make the gauntlet: a slightly flattened ball of silver clay with four holes. Three of them—the ones where you will need to put the index finger, the middle finger, and the pinkie—are in one direction. The hole for the thumb is in a direction opposite the three other holes.

44 Attach the gauntlet ball to the arm, and insert four silver clay worms into each hole, so that they stick out enough to be perceived as fingers. The fingers need to be a little chubbier than usual, because the knight's arm is an example of what is called a "velvet fist in an iron glove."

We have also added the large button to the outer side of the forearm with the help of some wire. When selecting a button for a shield, be careful not to go for an excessively large one. You do not want the shield to hide all the work you've put into the creature so far, unless, of course, yours is a rather cowardly knight, in which case, it even makes sense to have only the eyes and the top of the helmet sticking out from behind the button. You can use the size of the buttons you have available to determine the scale for your knight.

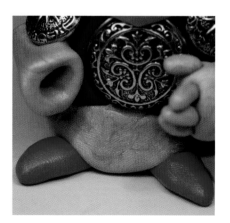

45 For the feet we chose two pieces of red clay, and pressed the body of the knight onto them. The choice of a warm color helps to brighten the color scheme, which until now was predominantly composed of different shades of blue and gray. Some golden buttons can also enhance the color scheme.

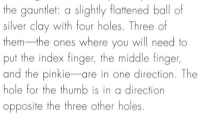

46 Using the cutters, cut a piece of old chain long enough to wrap around the neck of the critter. Make sure that the chain you are putting to a new purpose is in no way precious. Indeed, critter-making deserves some sacrifice, but the family's precious jewels should be spared.

47 Wrap the metal chain around the knight's neck, and gently push it in so that it slightly sinks into the clay and sticks on its own. Do the same with a different piece of chain (preferably more simple), about 1" (2.5 cm) long, only this time place it at the knight's waist, as a belt.

48 Before you bake the critter, the clay is usually sticky and holds the chains in place. After it hardens, though, the chains will most likely fall off. Therefore, we used the tiniest nails we could find, about 1/5" (5 mm) long, to fasten the chains to the critter for eternity.

49 Of all the medieval arms, the mace is the funniest, beyond any doubt. This humorous quality is why we chose to give the knight nothing but a huge mace that he cannot even lift.

Use the cutters to cut a 2" (5.1 cm) piece of chain (the simplest you can find). Run a 2" (5.1 cm) piece of wire through the last link, as shown.

50 Twist both ends of the wire around each other tightly. Put a flat piece of brown clay under the wire, and wrap the handle in it, covering half of the first link attached to the wire. This is the mace's handle, which the knight will hold.

51 Make a ball of silver clay about as big as the knight's head. Add a twisted bit of wire to the loose end of the chain (as you did for the handle). This time, make the wire somewhat shorter. Drive the twisted wire into the silver clay ball, and carefully squeeze around it to avoid ruining the oval shape of the ball. Prepare about 12 small silver cones to be the spikes of the mace. Add them as shown.

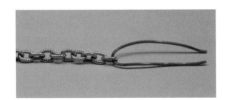

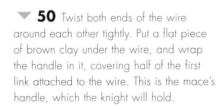

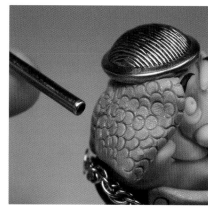

52 Now that we have the weapon, it would be good to make the hand that holds it. Roll four fingers from flesh or beige polymer clay, and insert them in the hole in the arm.

53 Place the handle of the mace in the hand, and wrap the fingers around it tightly. The end of the handle should touch the critter's body. It is a good idea to even make the handle sink a little bit into the blue clay—it will hold better that way.

The major sculpting work on the knight is over now. A few important last stages, however, still need to be completed. It is now time for decoration—drawing in the clay.

54 The objective here is to give the smooth clay surfaces some texture. To make the chain-mail parts of the helmet and the lower front part of the armor, use a tiny straw or any other object that creates small circles when you gently press it on the clay. We used a broken antenna bit. You can either place the circles next to each other or overlap them, which creates the illusion that the chain mail is composed of interwoven links. Put three little circles on the gauntlet, too.

55 Use the pin to draw some lines with little dots on one side to create the impression that the solid armor is composed of separate sheets of metal that are attached to each other. Draw a long line with cross-stitches on each foot, to make them look more like shoes. We added the same drawing on the knight's nose. Given his occupation, it seemed natural that he should have a scar or two. Draw a small goatee on the knight's chin, using the same method we used for the Easter Bunny's hair—make a horizontal line and perform a series of short, energetic, downward strokes with the pin.

Finally, make a deep hole next to the helmet button in which to insert a feather after you bake the critter. Do not put the feather in the oven.

Bake the knight following the clay manufacturer's instructions, and let it cool. For more tips on baking, see page 7.

56 Your knight is now finished, firmly anchored to the ground by his gigantic weapon.

Variation Ideas
Chubby Knight

This variation makes more extensive use of buttons and a heavy metal ring for a helmet. Making the knight's head smaller in proportion to the body makes him look more corpulent.

Knight with Chain Helmet

Here is a variation of the knight. We used short pieces of chain for the helmet instead of creating a dense circle texture. A paper clip bit in the club fulfills the function of armature.

TIP

Tin Foil

To make the ball of the mace lighter and save some clay, you can cover a ball of tin foil with a thinner layer of silver clay.

Cutting Chains

When cutting a chain, you will invariably sacrifice a link or two. Always make sure that the last link is closed, so that it can hold firmly to the wire bit that connects it to the clay.

Extra-strength Glue

Some of the buttons you attach with a piece of wire are likely to rotate or wobble after the critter is baked and the polymer clay is no longer sticky. Use a drop or two of any generic extra-strength glue to correct this problem. Extra-strength glue is also the best medicine for any broken clay parts.

We built an army!

THE WIZARD

One of the most popular fantasy characters is the wizard; usually an old bearded fellow with a pointy hat, a staff, and a magic crystal. Good or evil, wizards always have a lot of personality. This is the image we will try to capture in this lesson. The armature involved is quite simple, and we will practice embedding foreign objects in clay characters. This is the project in which we turn a marble into a magic crystal.

So put on your spell-proof helmet, and let's see what we can conjure up with some clay, a piece of wire, a bit from a chandelier, and an old marble.

MATERIALS

½ sheet flesh or beige clay
(we used Super Sculpey)

⅛ block glow-in-the-dark clay

⅛ block white clay

⅛ block black clay

1 block dark blue clay

1 block light blue clay

½ block red clay

¼ block yellow clay

⅛ block light brown clay

⅛ block dark brown clay

1 marble

1 hexagonal chandelier crystal/glass bead

15 ³/4" (40 cm) 0.7 mm copper wire

TOOLS

Small tapered-point clay shaper

Small cup-round clay shaper

Needle or safety pin

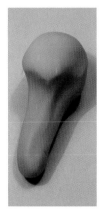

▶ **1** To make a shape like the one shown in the picture, roll a ball of clay and pull on one side of it. The oblong part will be the wizard's neck and the round one his head.

◀ **2** Perform the ingenious index-finger-and-thumb squeeze we have been using all along on the upper part of the head to generate the nose.

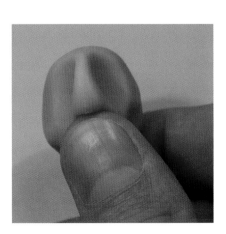

◀ **3** Push with your fingers, as shown, to define the length of the nose. A big nose has become an integral part of most wizard representations. Let's embrace this stereotype and bring it to a new dimension—forward, that is.

(Of course, you can go the nonconformist way and give this wizard a miniature, chipped nose. Then you can do away with the moth-eaten pointy hat and give him a baseball cap. And then you will have made a real wizard—one who has the ability to disappear! But what good is an invisible polymer-clay wizard? Doesn't everyone have tons of them in their closets? As you can see, this is getting slightly surreal, but such is our subject matter. Making a wizard is not for the weak at heart.)

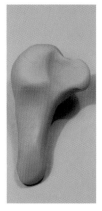
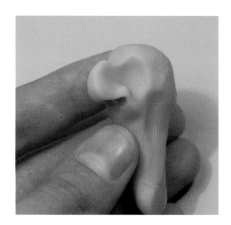

▲ **4** Our goal is to give the wizard a characteristic profile, so from the very first steps, we should make sure that the nose does indeed stand out.

▲ **5** With the tip of the tapered-point clay shaper, make holes for the nostrils. These holes should yield bumps on the outside of the nose.

▼ **7** Behold the nose you have created!

▲ **6** Outline the outer nostrils with the other clay shaper, pushing up with your thumb as shown to give the wizard flared nostrils. Flared nostrils contribute to a more intense facial expression.

▲ **8** Put your fingers on the critter's neck, and push forward and up with your thumb, as shown, to separate the wizard's chin from his neck.

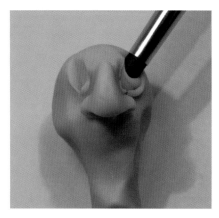
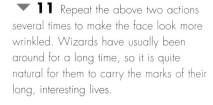

▲ **9** Stick the cup-round clay shaper into the head, and drag some clay down, as shown. The purpose of this move (and the next few) is to make eye sockets and create bags under the wizard's eyes.

▲ **10** Stick the cup-round clay shaper above the newly created shape and repeat the action, only this time, try to capture a larger quantity of clay.

▼ **11** Repeat the above two actions several times to make the face look more wrinkled. Wizards have usually been around for a long time, so it is quite natural for them to carry the marks of their long, interesting lives.

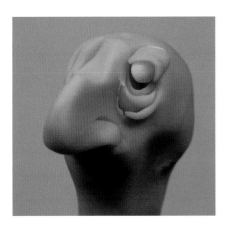

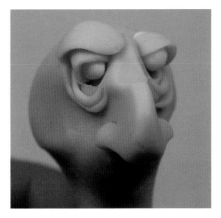

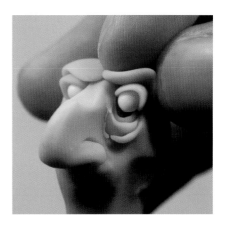

▲ 12 To make an eye, wrap a bead of glow-in-the-dark clay in flesh or beige clay, and place it on top of the uppermost eye bag, as shown. Leave a small hollow between the wrinkle and the eye to add to the magician's old age.

▲ 13 Cover one eye with an additional small piece of clay, on top of the inner part of the upper eyelid, to create the impression that the wizard is scowling.

▲ 14 Cover the other eye, too, only this time pinch the new piece of clay as shown. In doing this, we introduce an important asymmetry in the wizard's face—he looks as if he is raising an eyebrow. Raising an eyebrow is a widespread way of expressing powerful emotion among wizards.

▼ 15 Next, we will make the mouth. Insert the needle deep into the center of the face, right under and at a reasonable distance from the nose, leaving enough room for a big upper lip.

Using the tip of the needle as a lever, draw to one side and then the other to crack a smile on the wizard's face.

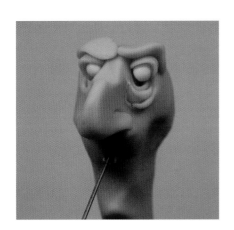

▶ 16 Here we used a random metal bit to open the mouth some more and then a clay shaper to widen it.

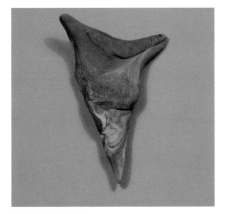

◀ 17 To create the beard, mix equal quantities of black and white clay, but do not knead until the color becomes uniform. We will use the half-mixed color to make a graying beard.

As for the shape of the beard, do not aim for perfection. The triangle you will make need not be perfect. This is only hair, after all, and as you know, hair is difficult to control and keep in order.

Note that the upper side of the beard triangle is a curve, which makes it easier to attach the beard to the face.

▲ **18** Attach the beard to the face, as shown. Now is also the time to insert a double or triple piece of wire through the neck, all the way into the head of the wizard. We are planning to make a tall critter, and he will need that rod of armature to keep him straight. We do not make any armature for the hands, because they will be close to the body.

▲ **19** Out of the same black-and-white mixture, make a snake with pointy ends and attach it under the wizard's nose as a moustache. Our moustache is in a bowlike shape, but you can have it in any configuration, as long as it doesn't stick out to the point that it will break off once the critter is baked.

Add thick eyebrows, as shown.

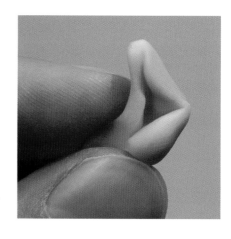

▼ **20** To make an ear, start with an irregular disk of clay. Then cut into it with your nail, as shown. Next, make a second cut vertical to the first one. Fold the clay along these cuts, and with your fingers sharpen the upper end of the ear, as shown.

Pointy elements are quite important when it comes to fantasy characters—pointy ears, pointy hats, pointy shoes, pointy fingers, and so on. Experiment with any creature you are making— add some pointy elements and see how it somehow acquires a fairy-tale-like quality.

 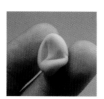 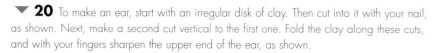

▲ **21** Before you finish the ear, make a small "joint," which will help us fasten it to the wizard's head. Extract this connecting bit out of the ear, as shown.

◀ **22** Stick the ear to the side of the head, and, using the tapered-point clay shaper, strengthen the bond.

▶ **23** This is what the ear looks like from the front. Note that it's quite large, relative to the nose.

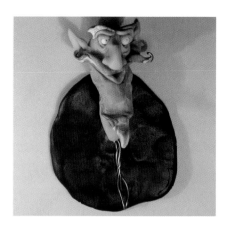

24 For the body of the wizard, make a thick, flat, elliptical shape of dark blue polymer clay, and place the head on top of it, as shown. To generate the volume of the body, wrap the wire bit and the neck in a dark blue burrito.

25 When you perform the wrapping procedure described in the previous step, use the top edge of the ellipse to give the wizard a collar. Have the back of the critter's neck stick to the blue "gown" (another word for burrito), but leave the whole collar slightly spread. Squeeze the blue clay tightly around the wire at the very end of the neck so that the flesh or beige clay and the blue clay can form a bond. Needless to say, the beard must be on top of the gown.

The base of the gown should be quite wide so that the wizard will be more stable.

26 To make a pointy hat, make a cone of dark blue clay by rolling a piece of clay between your palms. Then place the pointy hat on the wizard's head. From the back, the hat should almost touch the collar. Try to cover as much head surface as you can without touching the face. Bend the hat forward a little, if necessary, to restore the critter's weight balance.

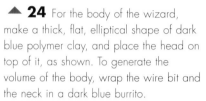

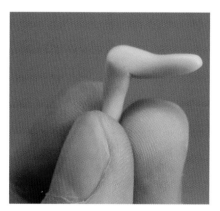

27 Use your thumb to put a dent on the wizard's torso. This is where you will soon insert the pointy end of a cone, similar to the one you made for the hat, which will be the wizard's sleeve. This time you'll make the cone of lighter blue.

28 Bend the sleeve into a 60-degree angle, and sharpen the elbow with your index finger and thumb.

29 Using flesh or beige polymer clay, make finger, like those shown in the picture; they are just rounded-end, right-angled clay worms.

▲ **30** With the tip of a tapered-point clay shaper, dig into the base of the sleeve cone to make a "nest" for the fingers.

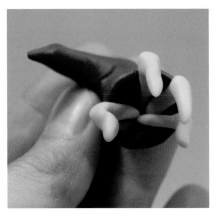

▲ **31** Insert the fingers into their nest by sticking two-thirds of the way into the inside of the sleeve, as shown. Notice how the thumb's upper part is slightly curved—this curve, in addition to its opposing position and its relative thickness, distinguishes the thumb from the other fingers. Make the tips of the other fingers a little pointier to increase the distinction between the fingers and the thumb.

▲ **32** Place a small marble in the wizard's hand. If you find a fancy marble, your wizard can only benefit, but even the most standard marbles—with the spirally thing inside—work great, because that spirally thing looks like a flame.

Group the three fingers so that their tips touch.

After baking the critter, apply a small drop of extra-strength glue between the marble—now promoted to a magic crystal—and the sleeve to keep the marble from rotating. The glue also makes the structure firmer.

▲ **33** Next we will make the wizard's staff. A staff is as essential to a wizard as a sword is to a knight.

We used a broken-off piece of a chandelier crystal, but if you don't have one handy, you can use a glass bead with a hole in it. Bend a piece of wire in two, and twist the ends around each other. Then run one of the ends through the hole in the crystal, as shown

▲ **34** Wrap a piece of light brown or gold-colored clay around the wire, and stick it firmly to the crystal. Try to cover the hole through which you ran the wire.

▲ **35** Roll a thin snake of dark brown clay, and squish it flat. Position it next to the double wire that forms the staff's backbone, and wrap the clay tightly around it.

36 Following the instructions for the wizard's left hand, make a right one. Place the staff in it, and wrap the fingers around the staff. Attach the left sleeve firmly to the body. Stick the staff to the outer side of the collar. You can stick the lower end of the staff into the "fabric" of the wizard's gown. The more possible contact points you can create between the wizard and his magical instrument the better, because the figure is less likely to break if it has more support.

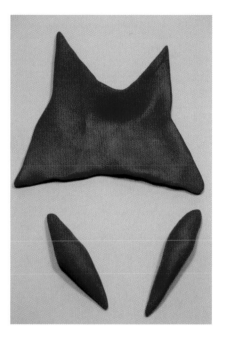

37 Using red clay, make a robe for the wizard with a shape roughly similar to that shown in the photograph. The two upper ends are supposed to go around the critter's neck.

Make two longish, pointy loaves of red clay for the critter's feet. Because the wizard is wearing a long robe, only his feet will be visible. Stick the wizard's body on top of the feet. The back of the feet may need to be squished flat by the bottom of the critter to maintain the wizard's balance.

38 Roll out a short, thin yellow snake with sharp ends, and stick it on the wizard's hat, as shown. Flatten it a bit but be careful not to ruin the sharp ends. Then make another tiny yellow snake, and stick it perpendicular to the first one so that they can form a star. Add more evenly spaced stars all over the wizard's robe and hat.

Do not make the snakes too thin because they will look green on the blue surface. When you flatten an overly thin piece of yellow clay on a dark blue surface, the yellow clay becomes almost translucent and, as you may know from basic color theory, blue + yellow = green.

39 Wrap the two upper ends of the cloak around the wizard's neck, below his collar. The center of the cloak should cling to the back of the wizard. You can play with the ends of the cloak to create the impression that the wizard is standing in the wind.

40 Use the needle to draw some individual hairs on the wizard's beard, moustache, and eyebrows. Squish a small ball of flesh clay flat, and insert it into the wizard's mouth using a clay shaper. Then, using the needle, inscribe a line in the center of the tongue.

41 Pinch the wizard's nose one last time to make it pointier.

42 With the needle, add some finishing touches to the face—draw wrinkles around the eyes, put some marks on the nose.

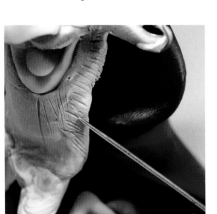

43 Roll out a small snake of flesh or beige clay, bend it into a moon shape, and attach it as a lower lip with the help of a tapered-point clay shaper. The lower lip makes the tongue appear more realistic.

◀ **44** Point the tips of the wizard's pointy shoes up to give the impression of better self-esteem. Adding a set of upper teeth is likely to produce a similar effect. Add a short snake of glow-in-the-dark clay right under the moustache, without covering the whole mouth, and use a needle to separate the individual teeth from each other, drawing toward the moustache.

◀ **45** Bake the wizard following the clay manufacturer's instructions, and let it cool. To be on the safe side, bake the critter lying on his back. Make cushions of tin foil to make it more comfortable and to prevent his posture from changing while in the oven. For more tips, on baking see page 7.

Or How to Make a Horse

This project provides another armature lesson, in which we will practice working with larger volumes of clay. The skills you will learn while making a horse are transferable to any four-legged character. Should you want to make a unicorn, for instance, all you have to do is make an emaciated white horse and put a horn in the middle of its forehead. If you want to make a tall two-legged critter with a tail, just think of it as a vertical horse.

MATERIALS

2 blocks light brown clay
¼ block dark brown clay
⅛ block glow-in-the-dark clay
¼ block white clay
39½" (1m) 0.7 mm copper wire

TOOLS

Wire cutters
Needle or safety pin
Small tapered-point clay shaper
Small cup-round clay shaper

▲ **1** Start with a piece of wire approximately 39½" (1 m) long. As we did in when making the dragon, we will make the armature of the creature from a single piece of wire. Because a horse should ideally have four legs, making its wire skeleton will require a few more steps, but the basic armature principle of the twisted double wire remains the same.

▲ **2** Fold the piece of wire in the center, and twist both ends around each other until you have approximately 4" (10.2 cm) of double wire. This structure will be the neck of our horse. Make sure to leave the loop sufficiently large because it will serve as the armature for the horse's head.

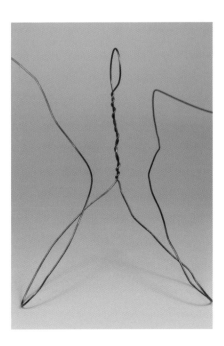

◀ **3** To make a leg, fold one of the two loose ends and twist it until the base of the neck. Once again, make sure to leave a loop at the end, around which we will build the hoof. You can make this loop small if you want your horse to be more graceful, although giving your horse big hooves will make it more solid, especially if it has one leg in the air. Excessively large hooves do not merely play a functional role; they are also essential in making the horse funnier. In this particular project we are going for an amusing horse that has one leg in the air.

Make another front leg.

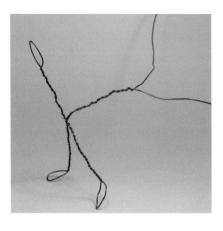

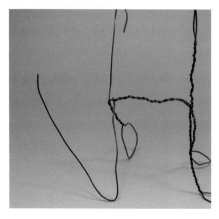

▲ **4** Twist the wires perpendicular to the neck and the front legs, working toward the rear legs. When you reach the desired length of this "spinal cord," bend the two loose ends down, fold them it half, and twist them back up to the horse's lower back.

▲ **5** We have left the loose ends sticking out to illustrate the fact that we do not use any additional wire for the armature. The main structure is finished now; the only remaining bit is the tail. To make the tail, twist the two ends around each other for the last time, and snip off the remaining single wire.

Raise one of the front legs, and bend it at the knee and at the ankle. This is a typical horse pose. (This could be a basic dog's pose, too. Consider making a dog based on the same armature as a possible extension of this project.)

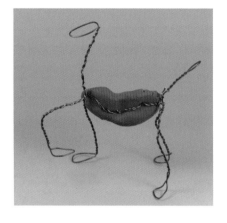

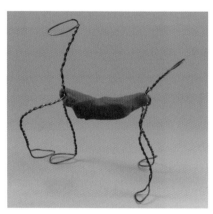

▲ **6** Once the armature is complete, we need to cover it. We will use just clay to create the volume of the horse. You can also use tin foil, especially if you are running short of clay or just want to make your horse lighter.

Using a piece of light brown clay, and proceed as shown.

◀ **7** In the same way, proceed with the other body parts, covering them with a first layer of clay. Bear in mind that the horse's torso should be somewhat thicker than his limbs. Repeat with a second, thick layer. Cover the head, too, using an oblong piece of clay that is slightly thinner toward the front and thicker toward the back.

▶ **8** The aspiring horse will look like an ostrich unless you make his neck thicker, too.

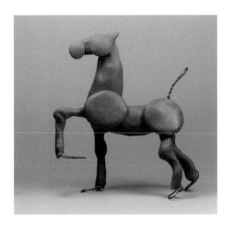

◀ **9** After all this covering with clay, the horse is a little flat and lacking in volume. To correct this and create the characteristic horse look, we will use the simplest geometrical shape—the circle. Out of several balls of clay, squish a few disks—four big ones for the horse's shoulders and hind legs, two medium ones for his cheeks, and two small ones for his nose. Stick these disks on both sides of the horse, as shown.

Ideally, these disks should be thicker in the center and thinner around the edges so that you can more easily blend them with their surroundings.

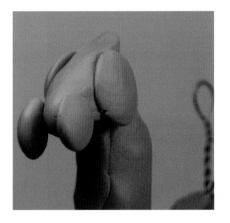

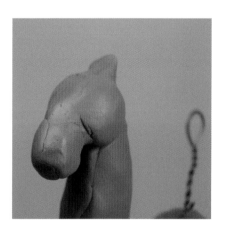

▲ **10** In this close-up of the head you can see why horses run so fast—clearly it is because their heads are apparently made of sports cars! Whether you find this logic compellingly persuasive or not, you will have to "hide" the car in the horse's head. To do this, gently smooth the periphery of the disk into the surrounding clay with your fingertip.

Pinch the back of the head with your index finger and thumb to create the impression of ears. We will add real ears later, but sometimes having a dummy body part on a critter helps you better see the direction in which things are going.

▲ **11** Apply the same smoothing technique to the other four disks. You will most probably end up with something that looks like the corner photo.

Notice that the hind legs bend backwards—it is as if this horse is actually a carnival costume with two men in it, men with huge knees. To avoid that illusion, just turn the horse's knee around. Now it looks as if it bends forward, which is somewhat closer to the true anatomy.

▲ **12** Here is what the horse looks like from the back. You can clearly see the shoulder volume and the volume of the buttocks, which was obtained by wrapping the disks around the previous thinned version of the horse.

◀ **13** At this stage, you need to make the horse's knees stand out. Tightly squeeze the clay above and below the wire inside the knees to make them more prominent.

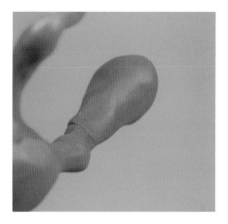

▲ ▶ **14** To give the horse hooves, wrap a chunk of light brown clay around the wire feet to create a funnel. The hooves should have a rough, conical shape, the tip of which merges in the legs.

▲ **15** It's time for another round of smoothing and blending. The disks you used for the horse's buttocks need to make one whole with the thin leg that was there before. Use a clay shaper to remove seams and smooth the areas that are hard to reach.

▲ **16** To ensure the horse is stable, make sure that when you look straight from the back though the hind legs of the horse the front supporting leg is more or less in the middle.

A horse standing on three legs may seem a little less stable on a level surface, but, in fact, it is more stable because, according to basic geometry, any three points can lie in one plane, while any four points cannot. This is also why photographers use tripods instead of quadripods.

▲ **17** To correct problems, such as irregular distribution of clay and overthinned legs, use small, flat pieces of clay to create volume layer by layer. Ideally, you should use as few layers as you can, because you'll run a lower risk of ending up with a critter that looks like patchwork. The best way to merge additional layers with the whole is with your fingertips. The finger method also ensures that the shape that you are building on and the shape that you are adding will have the same texture.

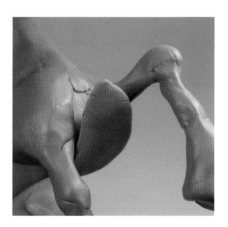

◀ **18** Add a new layer to the breast of the horse to make it look more powerful. That new layer should also be thicker in the middle with thinner edges.

▲ **19** A natural way of holding the horse while you work is by the torso (index finger on the back, thumb on the belly, or vice versa). Unfortunately, this grip is likely to have flattened it excessively. Add another thick layer to the horse's belly to make it a bit more swollen.

▶ **20** Wrap a piece of dark brown clay around the protruding wire tail. Fasten the clay part of this new tail firmly to the body, and arch it a bit. Hold the back of the horse's neck between your index finger and thumb, and with a series of short pinching moves, arch it a bit, too.

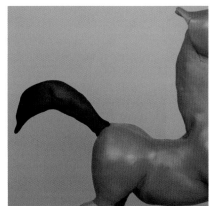

▲ **21** Use your fingernail to separate the hoof from the leg.

◀ **22** Now is the time to make sure that all of the hooves are the same size. Cut from the ones that are slightly bigger, and add to the ones that are smaller.

23 Back to the head. Fill the hollows between the horse's cheeks and under his nose with two small pieces of clay, using the tapered-point clay shaper to blend them with the rest of the head.

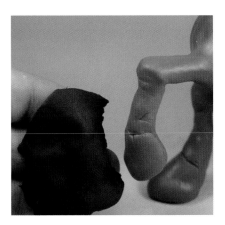

24 Make a thin, wide sheet of dark brown clay with which to cover the hoof. You may ask: "But why didn't we make the hooves out of dark brown clay in the first place?" Because we didn't think of it at the time. It is often impossible to plan everything in advance, so you have to make up things as you go. The most painless approach here is to cover the hoof with a thin layer of a different color, rather than take it out completely and replace it with a new one.

25 Our horse finally has shoes. Not horseshoes, though—only domesticated horses have horseshoes, and ours is a proud wild stallion. Besides, making horseshoes would be like nit-picking, so we'll leave that for the extra-zealous readers.

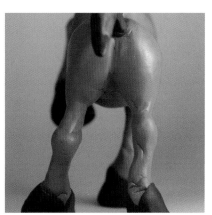

26 With the tip of your finger, smudge a little bit of the light-brown clay from the leg over the hoof. Make sure there are no air bubbles under the thin layer of dark brown clay. If there are any, poke a hole in them with the needle, and then gently press to flatten the bubble. Don't forget to cover the little hole.

27 Here is a general rear view of the horse. Note that his belly should be visible, as it is in the picture.

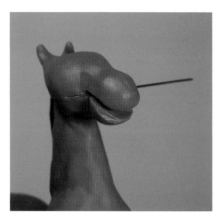

▲ **28** Add a band of dark brown clay along the back of the neck to give the horse a mane. Squeeze repeatedly with your index finger and thumb to attach it to the neck.

▲ **29** Open the mouth of the horse using a cutter blade or a needle.

▲ **30** Create holes to mark the prospective spots for the nostrils and the eyes. The eyes are usually wider apart than the nostrils.

◀ **32** Fill these holes with two beads of glow-in-the-dark clay. We didn't use eyelids this time, for a change, but you can always add them. The result is a horse with a less intense expression.

We also drew a few hairs on the forehead to experiment, but you won't see them in later steps.

▲ **31** Now, using the back of the clay shaper handle, make two holes into the head on top of the marks you created with the needle in the previous step.

◀ **33** Use the needle to underline the eye of the horse, as shown.

▶ **34** Remove the two dummy ears, and poke two holes in their place where you will next insert the real ears.

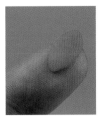

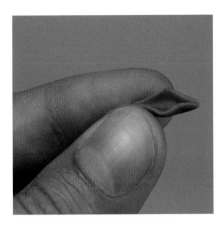

▲ **35** To make an ear, start with a small elliptical shape, and fold its ends until it starts looking like a boat.

▲ **36** Then insert the new ears in their respective holes, making sure they are well attached to the head. Continue the mane all the way to the forehead. Also widen the upper part of the nostrils, and make them slightly oblong.

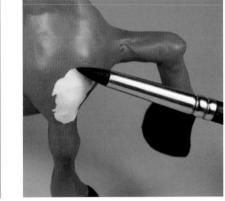

▲ **37** Fill the horse's mouth with tiny balls of clay, similar to the ones you used for the eyes. They will eventually become slightly rectangular as you push them. The lines you see going from the eyes down to the nose are another feature you can add.

▲ **38** Here is the head at this stage.

▲ **39** It's time to give this horse some pizzazz. Create some irregular, extra-thin patches of white clay (not glow-in-the-dark, but the opaque white), and distribute them here and there on the horse's body. Then, with a rolling motion of the tapered-point clay shaper, level the edges of the white patches. The white spots shouldn't stand out above the surface.

◀ **40** We thought it would be smart to put a white spot on the horse's forehead. Be careful not to overuse the small white patches, though—a horse is not the negative of a giraffe, nor does he have a skin condition.

◀ **41** Use the needle to draw some hairs on the horse's tail and on his hair. Notice the distribution of white patches we chose for the back of the horse.

◀ ▼ **42** Here is your finished beast of burden, er, I mean...noble animal!

Bake the horse a little longer than the clay manufacturer's instructions require at the appropriate temperature because a lot of clay went into this critter.

Variation Ideas
Mythical Unicorn

Making a unicorn is a direct and natural extension of the horse project, as we said earlier. Just remember to put a piece of wire in the horn.

Relaxing Giraffe

Four-legged animals need not always be standing up. Here is an example of how to make a giraffe sitting down in an almost human pose, using minimum armature. Notice how all his legs and tail are close to the body to minimize the potential risk of breaking.

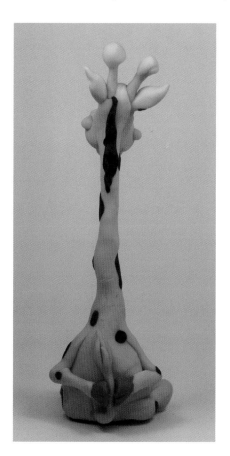

What the skeleton we will learn how to make in this project does best is meditate—the process of going out into the woods, sitting under a tree for seven years, and doing nothing but thinking. Our skeleton's power of concentration is so amazing that he even glows at night! Of course, that might have more to do with the glow-in-the-dark clay we will exclusively use in this project rather than with the skeleton's brainpower.

We will learn first how to make a skull, and then we will explore the possible ways of combining bones into a body. Skeletons can be thought of as jigsaw puzzles, made up of hundreds of parts that need to be put together. Our concern, however, is with a more stylized skeleton, almost made of flesh and blood, so we will merge many of these puzzle bits together.

1 block glow-in-the-dark clay
3" (7.6 cm) 0.7 mm copper wire
1 miniature straw hat (optional)

Small tapered-point clay shaper
Needle or safety pin
Wire cutters

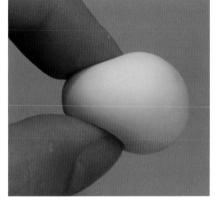

1 Make an egg shape or simply a ball by rolling a piece of clay between your palms. We used glow-in-the-dark clay because it has a nice bone color during the day. When you bake it really well (even if it turns slightly yellowish), it contributes to the true bone look of the skeleton.

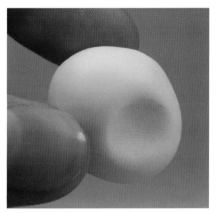

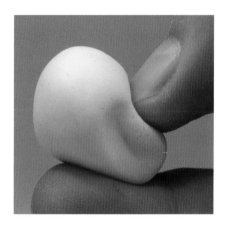

2 Squeeze half of the ball between your index finger and thumb, as shown. Refer to the picture to see the dents your fingers are supposed to leave on both sides of the skull. The idea is that a skull consists of an upper part—the cranium—which is round with a larger volume and a lower part—under the cheekbones and down to the lower jaw—which is more rectangular and generally narrower. We are now working on separating these two parts.

3 Push with your thumb on the back of the skull toward where the face will be. Exert counterpressure on the future face with your index or middle finger. You can use both hands if you find it easier. Just be sure to push with your thumb in a direction perpendicular to the face.

  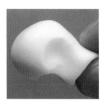  

5 After the first couple of steps, the side and front views indicate that the lower, square part of the skull should lie not directly under the upper round one but aligned on one side.

4 This is a view of the back of the skull. Notice the marks that your thumbnail left during the previous step. You can also clearly see the two shapes starting to form—the wider upper part and the smaller, square lower part.

6 This series of steps is aimed at sharpening the distinction between the lower "box" and the upper "ball" that make up the skull. With the tips of your index finger and thumb, gently squeeze each edge of the lower jaw to make it sharper.

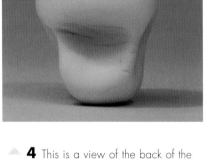 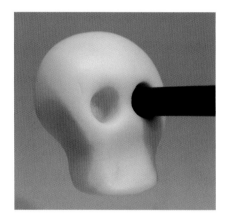 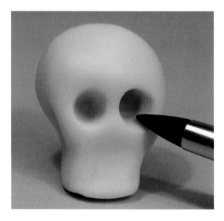

7 When you turn the skull upside down, the general box and ball distinction should be more or less visible. Right in front of you once again is the mark your thumbnail left on the back of the critter.

8 Using the clay shaper's handle, make two holes in the lower part of "the ball" for the eye sockets. These holes should be quite deep.

9 Use the tapered-point clay shaper, and, with a rotating motion, smooth the lower edges of the eyes sockets toward the cheekbones.

10 To make the temples, squeeze the forehead very gently between your index finger and thumb. Be careful to preserve the volume of the back of the head.

This move should have helped the cheekbones stand out.

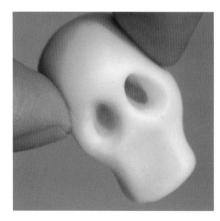

11 Push down on the side of the eye sockets to make the cheekbones even more prominent.

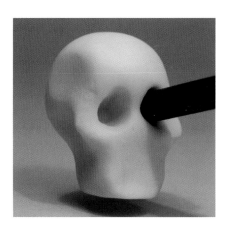

12 Stick the clay shaper handle into the eye sockets again to make them round—the previous procedures have probably distorted them somewhat. Notice this action's result on the cheekbones.

13 Drive the needle deep into the clay, and draw an inverted "V" to make the nose of the meditating skeleton. Think of it as writing—you need to go from left to right, without extracting the needle.

We are using only one color of clay for this project, so to shape the critter, we have to rely on the contrasts that occur when we create volume and draw in the clay. This is why we made the eye sockets, a few steps ago, and the nose so deep.

14 Make two balls of glow-in-the-dark clay small enough to sink to the bottom of the eye sockets.

A skull is by definition a scary dead head, but in this project the objective is to make a skull that defies that definition, a skull that looks alive and funny. Therefore, you have to give it real eyeballs to fill the hollows in his head. (Think of it as a biological paradox, just like the belly button of the bird.)

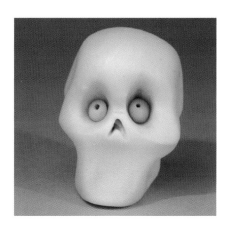

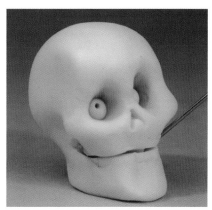

15 Insert the eyeballs into the sockets, and poke a hole in each one with the needle. You can also stick the ball on the tip of the needle first and then put it into the eye socket. Either way the result should be the same.

16 Skeletons have a reputation of always smiling. No doubt it must be easier for them. To allow our skull live up to the conventional standards, draw a huge smile on his face, starting from the side, as shown.

17 Make a mouth corner/cheek, just like the ones you made for the majority of the projects so far. This time, the mouth corner should be quite small to preserve the "ball and box" distinction. Add the corners to the skull.

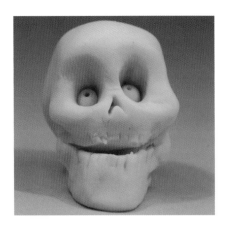

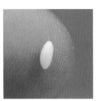

18 Use the pin to open the mouth a bit, and draw vertical lines on the upper and lower jaws to create the impression of teeth.

19 Make a couple of small grains of clay, as shown, and randomly add them to the lower and upper jaws. Our skull, perfect in every other respect, will have a couple of missing teeth.

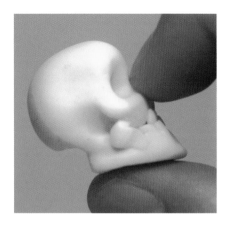

20 To give the skull a nicer profile, carefully push with your fingernail above the nose and between the eyes.

21 Here is the finished skull after the sculpting phase. Notice how the irregularly positioned teeth, the needle marks, and the actual clay bits complement each other to create the dental impression. Pinch the skull's chin to make it pointier.

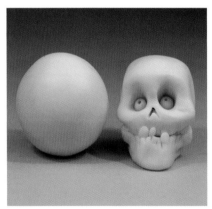

22 Skeletons are often said to be quite skinny. This, however, need not always be the case, and for this project you will learn how to make a fellow with a belly. For a start, roll a ball slightly larger than the skull.

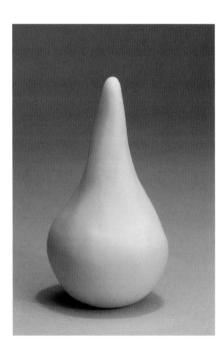

23 Rolling the ball between your fingers to elongate one end until the ball resembles a bulb. The tapered end will be the neck of the skeleton and the lower round end the torso.

  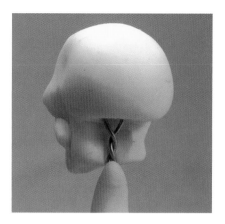

24 To create the armature, bend 3" (7.6 cm) of wire in two, and twist both ends around each other.

25 Stick the armature bit in the skeleton's body where the neck starts, and push it into the clay along the height of the neck. The loop of the armature bit should be on top; it will go into the skull.

26 Cover the wire with the surrounding clay, leaving just the loop and the first twist naked. Carefully push the skull onto the wire neck until the wire disappears and the clay of the neck touches the lower jaw and the bottom of the cranium. Use the clay shaper to strengthen the clay joints between the skull and the neck.

27 Here is the skeleton's profile so far.

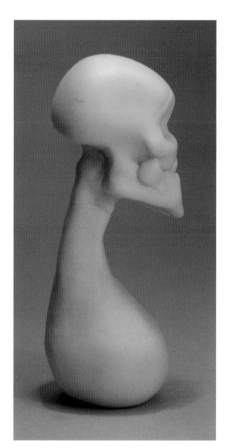  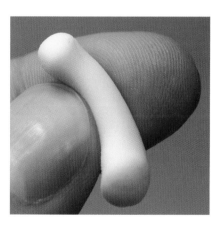

28 Now that you have the torso and the head, you need some limbs. To have some limbs, you need some bones. To have some bones, you will need to make them, starting with a small ball of glow-in-the-dark clay.

29 Roll the clay back and forth between your index finger and thumb until you have a shape with two "heads." To achieve such a shape, just hold the ball by the equator while rolling. You may find it easier to roll with the side of your fingertips rather than the center.

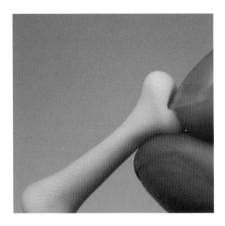

30 With the tip of your nail, cut into the oval end, as shown.

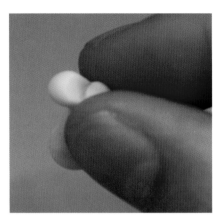

31 Holding the bone vertically, carefully squeeze the part that was just under your nail, not with the intention of flattening it but to restore the original width of the shape, which was slightly increased in the previous step.

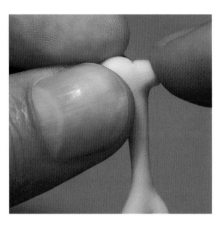

32 Holding the bone horizontally, push down a bit on one of the joints.

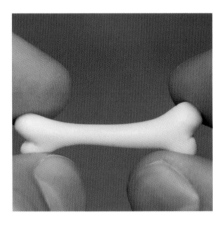

33 Here is the finished bone. You can gently pull on both ends to make it longer, but be careful because doing this will make the bone thinner as well. Proceed similarly with the rest of the bones.

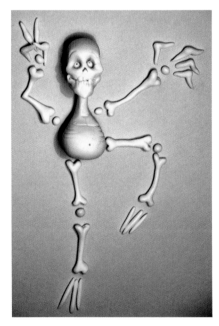

34 The first specimen of this type of skeleton was found after long and reluctant archaeological excavations somewhere very far away. The pose in which he was found suggests that he must have had interests other than meditation, for he was found in a ballet position, making a victory sign with his right hand. Nevertheless, scientists were able to decipher the map of his body and reconstruct him to the last detail.

We will use that same map to make our skeleton. Apparently, we need, all in all, six bones, six toes, eight fingers, two balls for the kneecaps, two for the shoulders, and two for the wrists.

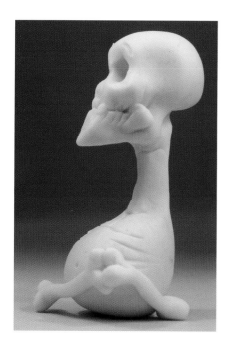

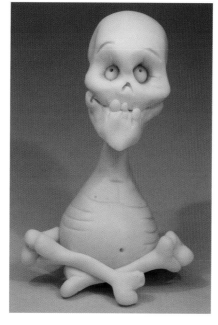

35 The skeleton will be sitting cross-legged in a typical meditative position. Firmly attach two of the bones to the body, as shown. The back end of the rear leg bone should be sticking to his bottom. The middle of that bone should be attached to the side of his body, and the other end should be attached to the front leg bone. The front leg bone's middle is attached to the critter's belly. Try to have as much contact surface between the bones and the body as possible, so that the skeleton will be less likely to break.

36 Repeat the same steps for the other leg. This time, the front leg bone is attached to the belly and to the front leg bone of the other leg.

At this point we were tempted to give the skeleton ribs, a belly button, and a chest, as well as eyebrows, using the needle. This drawing stage can take place at any moment of the critter-building process, although it usually comes last.

37 To add feet to the skeleton, first connect the three toes of each foot together, and then stick them to the lower ends of the front leg bones and under the knees, as shown. Once again, try to maximize the contact surface.

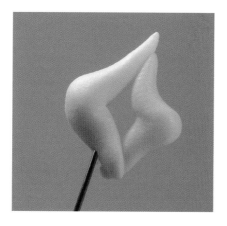

38 This is the index finger and thumb of the skeleton's hand. Stick their tips and bases firmly together. You will next attach them to the arms of the skeleton, for which we have already made the bones.

97

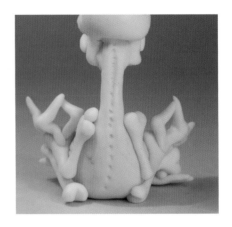

39 The arm of the skeleton is a bone that is simply bent in the middle and attached at shoulder height. It should follow the torso, with the forearm resting on the skeleton's thigh. The wrist should almost rest on the knee.

Attach the combination of index finger and thumb that you just made to the back of the skeleton's hand, as shown.

40 Turn the critter around, and add the other fingers, paying meticulous attention to how well they are attached to the bones of the hand and the knees. Because we do not use any armature for the arms and legs, it is to be expected that the fragile skeleton would not survive a nosedive from your work surface to the floor. However, we still have to ensure that the skeleton's parts do not come off in the morning breeze.

Add the small balls of clay for the kneecaps, the foot joints, and one of the shoulders. Leaving the other shoulder without a small ball makes the skeleton appear as if not all of his parts were found, which makes a more credible critter.

41 Trace the backbone using the clay shaper.

44 The last thing to do when making a skeleton is to turn off the lights to see if he has reached the desired level of enlightenment from his meditation practices.

Bake the character following the clay manufacturer's instructions, and let it cool. For more tips on baking, see page 7.

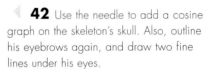

42 Use the needle to add a cosine graph on the skeleton's skull. Also, outline his eyebrows again, and draw two fine lines under his eyes.

43 In this optional step, weave a miniature straw hat, and place it on the skeleton's head after you have baked him.

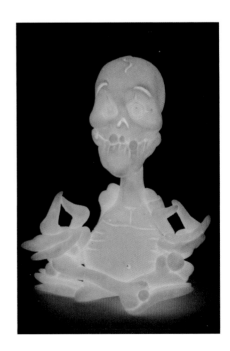

TIP

Regular White Eyeballs

To achieve a different glow-in-the-dark effect, you can make regular white clay eyeballs. Then two dark holes for the skull's eyes will appear when you turn off the lights.

Variation Ideas

Bird Skeleton

This chubby bird skeleton is largely made following the bird lesson. The only alterations are the use of glow-in-the-dark clay, the creation of deep eye sockets, and the use of a structure similar to that of the skeleton's feet for the wings.

Quadruped Animal Skull

Animal skulls are generally more elongated and have other bony bits protruding from their surface, such as horns. Prominent cheekbones and excessively large teeth are a must. You can also put two holes in the upper part of the forehead to make ear sockets.

Skeleton with a Ball and Chain

Making a skeleton with a ball and chain is a natural extension of the skeleton project. Creating the ball and chain is essentially the same process as the one we used to make the knight's mace. Be sure that the leg bone to which the chain is attached is a little thicker, because it will have to host the wire attachment.

Ghoulish Gang

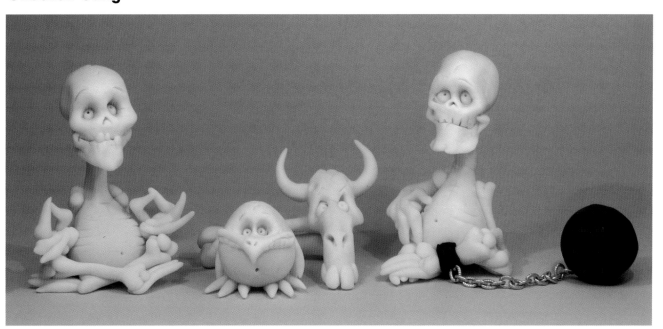

Whether Santa is an imaginary character or a real one has long been a subject of debate. In my opinion, he is the only *real* creature I could not resist including in this book.

The Santa character is made exclusively of clay—no armature and no embedded objects go into him. You will learn how to make a generic Santa, complete with a red coat, a Christmas tree, and a present, but if you are creating him in the middle of July, feel free to give him a pair of shorts and flip-flops.

MATERIALS

1 block red clay
½ block flesh or beige clay
⅛ block glow-in-the-dark clay
1 block white clay
¼ block dark green clay
⅛ block brown clay
¼ block yellow clay
⅛ block pink clay

TOOLS

Small tapered-point clay shaper
Small cup-round clay shaper
Needle or safety pin

▲ **1** Red polymer clay is the messiest color of them all. The pigment in the red clay tends to color your fingers when knead it, and unless you are working next to the sink and washing your hands every two seconds, you are likely to leave red fingerprints all over the other light-colored polymer clays you use. It is strongly recommended that you first complete the red bits of the character and then move on to all the rest.

Start with a ball of red clay that will form the body of Santa.

▲ **2** With your thumb, press on the upper end of the ball to create a shape like the one in the photograph. The head will soon lie here; the thin, elongated upper end will be the collar of Santa's coat. The round part will be his belly.

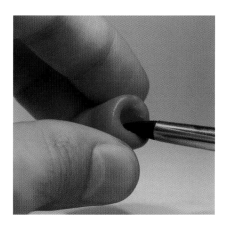

▼ **3** Make three conical shapes of red clay. Two of them, the arms, should have a smaller base, be slightly higher, and be bent in the middle. The third one, for the hat, should be straight and somewhat shorter, with a larger base.

◀ **4** With a rotating movement, use the tapered-point clay shaper to make holes in the bases of the arms. We will insert the fingers in these holes later.

You can wash your hands now; we are done with the red clay for the moment.

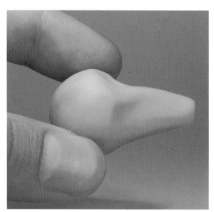

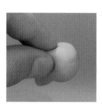

5 Roll a ball of flesh or beige clay a little bit smaller than the one you made for the body. Then, holding it with the fingers of your left hand, as shown, pull on one of the ends to elongate it.

6 This is roughly the shape you should have obtained after the last step. The round part will be the head, and the long, narrow part will be the neck, which will serve two functions—first, it will provide a holding place while you are working on the face, and second it will connect the critter's body to the head.

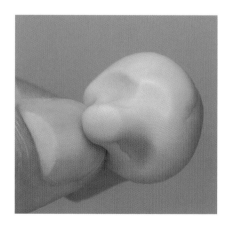

7 Perform an index-finger-and-thumb squeeze on the head to start extracting the nose. Make sure there is a fair amount of clay between your fingers, because Santa should ideally have a big nose. The line going from the end of the nose that you see in the picture is unintended, but we will not bother to remove it.

8 After the vertical squeeze, make a horizontal one. Then, using the nose as an axis, rotate the head, making a series of short squeezes, until you get a shape like this one.

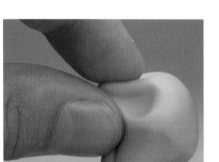

10 Push horizontally until your thumbnail defines the lower end of the nose.

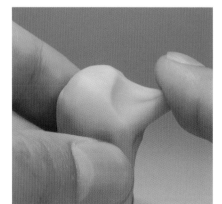

9 Clearly, if the nose keeps up its expansion, our critter will look more like Pinocchio than Santa. Push the nose back to make it rounder and bulkier.

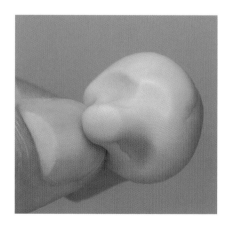

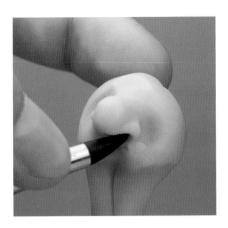

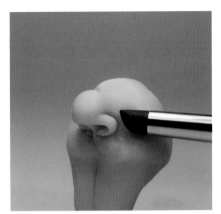

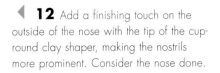

12 Add a finishing touch on the outside of the nose with the tip of the cup-round clay shaper, making the nostrils more prominent. Consider the nose done.

▲ **11** A nose, as we have seen before, traditionally consists of a protruding bit, the holes of the nostrils, and the outer nostrils. Here, as usual, we take care of the nostrils in one step. Stab the protruding bit with the tip of the tapered-point clay shaper, as shown, to generate the inner and outer nostrils.

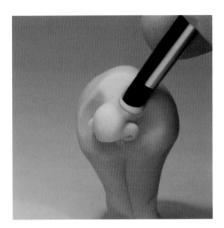

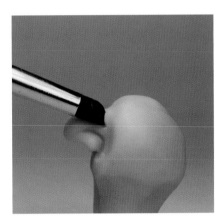

▲ **13** Using the round-cup clay shaper, prepare the ground for the eyes, as shown. Repeat this action to make the ripples of clay for the bags under the eyes.

▼ **15** A beard is actually made of a white croissant. To make the croissant, use off-white clay rather than sparkling white to minimize the risk of red fingerprints showing (see tip on page 108 for directions on making off-white clay). The croissant should have some volume.

▼ **14** Using the clay shaper's handle, open wide the critter's mouth. Don't worry, he won't be screaming the whole time—just until we give him a beard and moustache. Make two eyes of glow-in-the-dark polymer clay wrapped in flesh or beige clay, and insert them in their appropriate places.

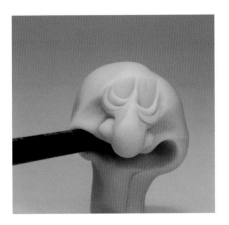

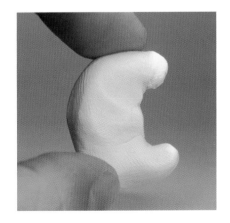

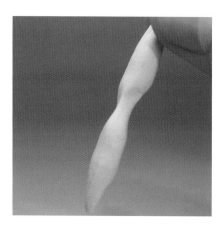  

16 To make the moustache, roll a snake of clay, making the middle thinner than the rest. This part will go under the nose, and we want Santa to be able to breathe.

17 Attach the beard to the head, with the ends of the croissant pointing up.

18 Then add the moustache, curving the ends around the cheeks. You may have to adjust the thinness of it.

19 With the tips of your index finger and thumb, gently squeeze, as shown, to create the pointy ends of the moustache. Then push with your thumb on the sides of the face to make the cheeks stand out. The moustache and beard are just hair that covers the face and should, therefore, follow some general facial features, which is why we still need to create a volume that can be interpreted as cheeks. Finally, push the croissant toward the nose to close the mouth.

20 To make the ears, take a small bit of clay, as shown, and fold it in half.

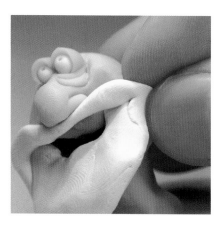 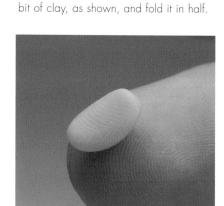

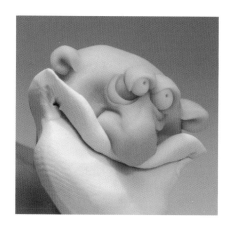

21 Attach the ear to the head, and using the tapered-point clay shaper, blend the upper part of the ear into the side of the head. The head is mostly done now, and we will return to the costume.

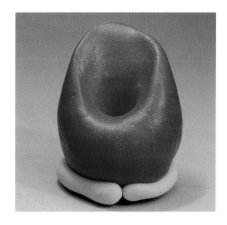

▲ 22 Using the clay shaper's handle, make a hole in the body where you will put the head. Hold the body with your left hand while making the hole with your right one.

▲ 23 Using your right hand, roll a snake of white clay with round ends to decorate the lower part of the coat. All these right hand/left hand instructions can help you avoid leaving red fingerprints and making fewer trips to the sink. If you are left-handed, just do the reverse, making sure to use different hands for the red and white clays.

▲ 24 Wrap the white snake around the lower edge of the coat, as shown, until the two ends meet at the front. If the white touches the working surface, Santa will appear to be wearing a long coat. If the white snake is at the "equator" of the belly, it will seem as if he is wearing some sort of pants.

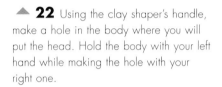

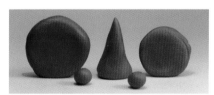

▲ 27 Now for the Christmas tree. Using dark green polymer clay, make a big disk, a medium disk, and a small base cone. The two little green balls will be the "stairs" between the different "floors" of the Christmas tree.

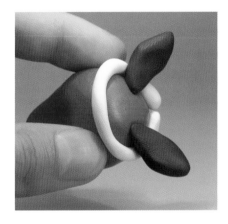

▲ 26 Attach the head to the body, putting the neck into the hole you made. If the neck is too long to fit, you may have to shorten it. So far, we have a Santa with a body and a head. We just need to give him arms. He needs arms to hold stuff, but we need to put that stuff on first and then put the hands around it.

▲ 25 Make two loaves of brown clay for the feet, and attach them to the body, as shown. The feet should be apart, because they will serve as props for the objects Santa will be holding.

▲ **28** Squeeze the two disks repeatedly while rotating them, as shown, to give them an irregular shape. Your squeezes should not overlap each other. Do the same to the base of the cone.

▲ **29** The idea, as you have probably already guessed, is to build the Christmas tree layer by layer: layer one, the big disk; layer two, the medium disk; layer three, the small base cone. To connect the layers, add one of the small green balls between each layer.

▲ **30** To complete the tree, make a hole on the bottom of the big disk, and insert a small brown polymer clay peg in it. The trunk of the tree has a purely functional role to play—it will not be too visible on the outside, but it will help fasten the tree to the body.

▲ **31** Stick the lowest layer of the tree above the white snake on Santa's coat, making sure to achieve maximum contact surface. The trunk should end up at the corner where the foot joins Santa's bottom.

▲ **32** Use the clay shaper's handle to make a hole at shoulder height where you will soon put the arm holding the tree.

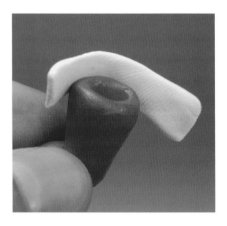

▲ **33** Wrap a flat, rectangular white sheet of clay around one of the prefabricated arms to make a cuff. Make sure that the two ends of the white cuff are close to each other.

34 Roll three short, chubby clay worms for the fingers and one for the thumb, and insert them in the sleeve, as shown, fastening them to the white and the red clay simultaneously.

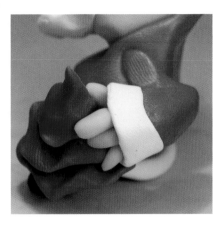

35 Attach the arm to the body, as shown. Each finger should rest on the tree, and the upper part of the arm should stick to the torso.

36 Let's give Santa a white collar. Roll a white snake with two pointy ends long enough to wrap around the critter's neck. Add it to the neck, starting from the front, as shown.

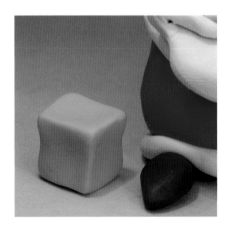

38 Roll a very thin snake of pink polymer clay, and wrap it around the box, as shown. Press on it lightly until it flattens. Do the same in the perpendicular direction, so that the pink ribbon forms a cross on the top of the present.

37 Santa usually carries a big bag full of presents for everyone, but our Santa will have a more personal approach—he'll be carrying just one present, for you. Make a cube of yellow polymer clay. If your cube does not have straight lines, don't bother to straighten them; you can always blame it on the wrapping paper.

39 Attach the packed present to the body and the foot.

40 Proceed with the right arm, similar to the way you did the left one, and wrap it around the present as well as you can, without covering too much of it.

41 The making of the hat is very much like the making of the arms. Wrap a piece of white clay around the wide end and set it on the head. In the picture you can see we played with the position of the tip of the hat. Give Santa a nice big white pompom on the end.

This is also the step in which you add the buttons to Santa's coat. Draw a line with the needle to indicate where the coat is buttoned. Then put several white disks of clay along that line. Push lightly with the clay shaper's handle in the center of each disk to form a small circular dent, and poke four buttonholes in a square formation in the center of each button.

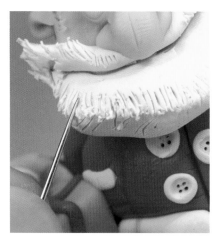

42 Use the tip of the needle to draw hairs on the beard and the moustache. You can draw the hairs on the edges of the beard to create a fuzzy impression.

This is also the time to draw wrinkles near the bottom-outer corners of the eyes. Add corners to the mouth and eyebrows on the white band of the hat. Draw a pocket on the coat, next to the present, and put a white bit on top of it to create the impression of an elaborate costume. Make some vertical marks on the Christmas tree, and draw a patch in the very center of the hat.

You are almost finished. The last thing to do is to decorate the Christmas tree—just put small, multicolored clay balls all over it. Bake Santa following the clay manufacturer's instructions, and let him cool. For more tips on baking, see page 7.

TIP

Off-White and Sparkling White

To make an off-white color for the beard, you can mix some flesh or beige clay with some sparkling white clay. The flesh or beige clays do not have enough pigment to drastically change the white color, but they can mute it a little bit.

The Universal Hat of Santa

This is probably obvious, but you can put small red-and-white Santa hats on all the ordinary critters you didn't give away before the start of the Christmas season to turn them into very appropriate Christmas gifts.

Variation Ideas
The Christmas Tree Has Had Enough

Now that you know how to make a Christmas tree, you just need to give it a face, some arms, and an ax to make it come to life. When making the trunk, use a cone with a wider base rather than a cylindrical shape so that your tree can stand firmly on its feet. We use short pin as armature for the ax's handle.

A More Earthly Santa

To make a Santa with some real purchasing power, place a coin in one of his hands and a bag with a patch in the other. The pom-pom is bigger this time, and we used a short piece of wire to connect it to the hat. You can also put a dollar sign on the sack instead of a patch to emphasize the point you are making.

Santa Imposter?

TRUTLIO THE TROLL

In this penultimate lesson you will learn one of the ways to make a troll-like creature. Very little is known about some imaginary characters, and we should say no more to maintain the air of mystery that surrounds them. This moth-covered cave dweller is a silent fellow, too, so he will appreciate the "don't ask, don't tell" approach, I am sure.

MATERIALS

½ block light green clay
¼ block light blue clay
⅛ block glow-in-the-dark clay
⅛ block dark brown clay
7" (17.8 cm) 0.7 mm copper wire

TOOLS

Small round-cup clay shaper
Needle or safety pin
Small tapered-point clay shaper
Wire cutters

▲ **1** Start with an egglike ball of clay. We mixed green and light blue clay in random proportion to obtain the green skin color with a shade of blue that you can see in the picture. Just like we did for the wizard's beard, we didn't knead the clay all the way but stopped before the color was uniform.

▲ **2** With your index finger and thumb, pinch the upper part of the egg. The clay between the two dents should be thick, because our goal is to give the troll a big nose.

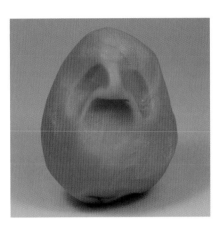

▲ **3** With your thumb, push the egg inward and upward. The mark this operation left on the critter's face is shown in the picture.

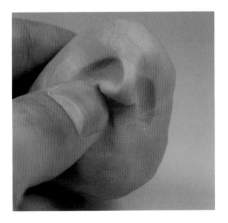

▲ **4** Push on the side of the nose again with your thumb to raise the nostrils slightly higher than the tip of the nose.

▲ **5** This is what the profile of the creature looks like.

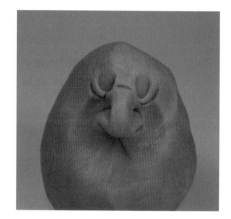

▲ **6** Using the cup-round clay shaper, outline the nostrils from the outside.

▲ **7** Also using the cup-round clay shaper, make the bags under the troll's eyes. With the tip of the clay shaper, leave a mark almost connecting the two eyes.

▼ **9** Put a third flat piece of green clay over the eyelids, as shown. The crease between this extra piece of clay and the eyelid creates the impression of an eyelid.

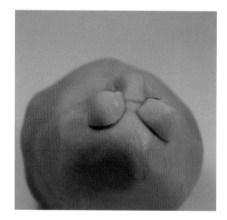

▲ **8** Wrap a small bead of glow-in-the-dark clay in a tiny sheet of green clay to make an eye. Notice that for the left eye we have first wrapped the bead in a dark blue piece of clay and then in green.

◀ **10** Push horizontally with your thumbnail to separate the head from the body. This separation will not be too radical, because we will not be giving the critter a neck, but it is still be helpful to know where his head ends so that you can appropriately place his facial features.

▶ **11** With the tips of your fingers, make the troll's jaw slightly ovoid.

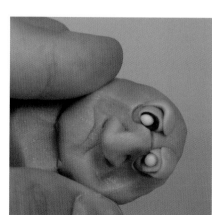

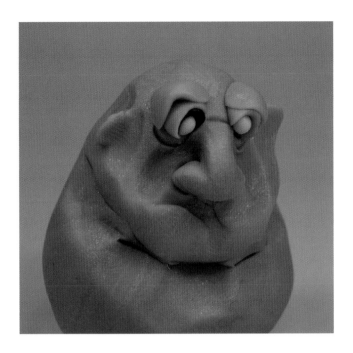

▲ **12** Gently pinch the sides of the troll's head with your fingers to produce two small ears. Our troll will have two delicate ears to contrast with his bulky persona.

▲ **13** Use the needle to open the mouth.

▼ **16** Press with your thumb on the lower jaw, as shown, to make the lower lip stand out.

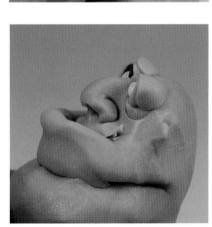

▲ **14** Make two holes for the troll's nostrils using the tapered-point clay shaper.

▲ **15** Add an additional flat sheet of green clay on the lower jaw to reinforce it. Smudge the right and left ends of it into the critter's face.

▶ **17** Here is the profile of the troll so far. The lower lip is slightly forward, and the ends of the additional flat piece of clay blend perfectly with the head.

19 Stick both wire legs into the critter, and check again whether he can stand on his feet. Ideally, he should be able to, but do not fret if he does not. You will add toes and heels to the wire armature later, which will stabilize it.

18 We will leave the troll's head alone for now and will turn to his legs. To produce humorous effect, we will give the troll short, skinny legs and giant feet. To do this we need armature. Bend a short piece of wire in half, and twist both ends around each other, as shown. A good leg armature should be able to stand straight without any help. Notice that the upper ends of the wire legs are slightly spread. This ensures that the leg will not rotate much when we stick it into the body, which is what we are about to do.

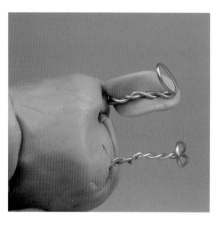

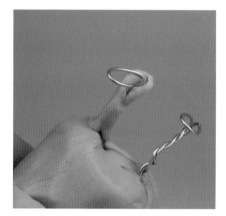

20 But let's make the legs first. Take a short, flat piece of clay, lay it next to the wire bit, and wrap it around the wire, as shown.

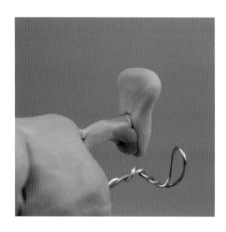

21 Next, cover the foot using the same technique, adding some more clay in the front for the toes and in the back for the heels.

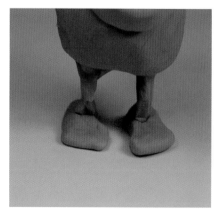

22 Here is what the feet look like at this stage. They look as if the troll has been wearing a pair of socks until they turned green to match the color of his skin.

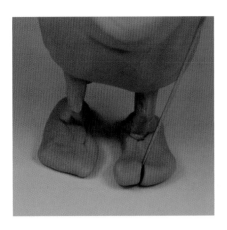

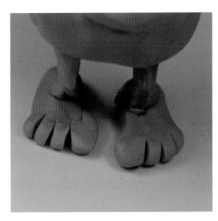

23 To correct this false impression, use the needle to separate the individual toes on the creature's feet. Then very carefully pull the toes apart.

25 Squeeze one end of the worm until you have a shape, as shown.

24 Now that our creature can walk, let's give it hands so that it will be able to carry things. To make an arm, start with a worm three times thicker than the troll's leg.

26 Then squeeze the new shape vertically until you get a finger.

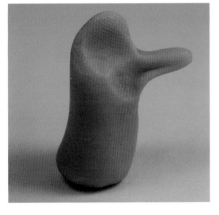

28 One problem you might run into is not enough clay at the end of a chubby clay worm to squeeze three fingers and a thumb. Look closely at the picture to find the answer: For the pinkie you have to start a lot lower than you did for the other fingers.

27 Making the other fingers is essentially the same—first squeeze horizontally, then vertically.

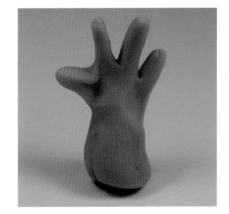

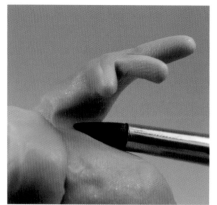

29 Attach the hand firmly to the troll's body, as shown. Then using a clay shaper, strengthen the bond and smooth the seams. Raise the other arm of the troll, as if he is making a gesture of some sort. Do not arrange the fingers on the hands in any particular configuration; the random position of the fingers will make the creature look clumsier.

30 Next, give the troll two chubby cheeks—clay worms with bulky middles and pointy ends. Smudge the ends into the surrounding face, thus integrating the cheeks into the happy family of the facial features.

31 This is what the face looks like so far.

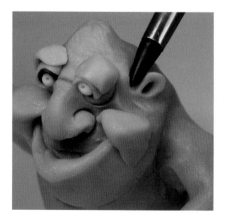

32 To add more detail to the ears, first poke a hole in it with the tip of the tapered-point clay shaper. Then, with the same tool, push both from above and below, as shown in the picture, to finish the ear.

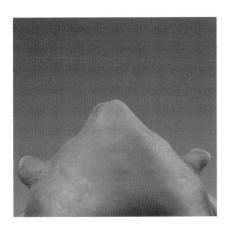

▲ **33** As you can see, our chubby, pointy-headed creature is still bald.

▲ **34** To remedy this condition, add a piece of dark brown clay to the very top of the critter's skull. Then draw some individual hairs on the small tuft of hair, keeping your finger on top of it so that it doesn't move.

▼ **35** Next, use the needle to draw a couple of wrinkles on the troll's forehead and to give him a pair of dimples. Also, make several marks in the critter's mouth to create the impression of teeth.

▼ **36** Put a disk of clay on the front of the troll to make his chest and belly. The disk should be thick in the middle, narrowing toward the ends.

▼ **37** Give the troll a belly button, and draw a chest for him. With the clay shaper's handle, make two small dents under each arm for armpits. Attach small oval pieces of clay as kneecaps and elbows.

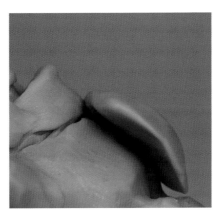

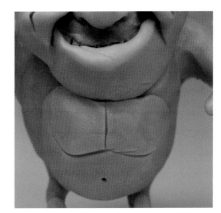

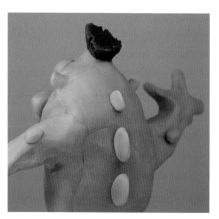

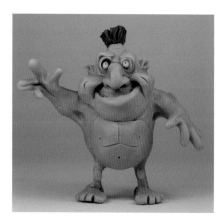

▲ **39** Put three oval pieces of clay on the back of the critter along the spinal cord to emphasize his nonhuman aspect. (Who knows, perhaps this troll is somehow related to the dragon we made earlier.)

▲ **40** You just finished your troll! He is waving his hand to say good-bye, because very shortly he will be off to take care of some highly important troll business.

▲ **38** Here is the profile of our fellow after we gave him a bigger belly.

▶ **41** Try talking the troll into sticking around for a few more minutes until you manage to slip two glow-in-the-dark teeth in his mouth when he is not looking.

Bake Trutlio following the clay manufacturer's instructions, and let him cool. For more tips on baking, see page 7.

Variation Ideas
The Beach Troll
This beach troll's neck is so thick that the golden chain around it broke—and it was the biggest size he could find in the troll jewelry store!

An Advanced Character
This greedy goblin gambler, who hasn't seen land for months, is very eager to multiply the treasures he has amassed. He is also an example of a more complex project, not because it involves things you do not yet know how to do, but because it involves *everything* you have learned in this book so far or knew intuitively all along.

MATERIALS

½ block beige clay

¼ block light blue clay

⅛ block light brown clay

⅛ block orange clay

⅛ block glow-in-the-dark clay

⅛ block white clay

½ block dark blue clay

½ block black clay

¼ block dark brown clay

¼ block red clay

⅛ block yellow clay

59" (1.5 m) of 0.7 mm copper wire

Tin foil

4 rings: 1 large, 2 medium, and 1 small

2 pieces of an old chain, 2" (5.1 cm)

TOOLS

Wire cutters

Small tapered-point clay shaper

Small cup-round clay shaper

Needle or safety pin

Sharp blade

▼ **1** Start with an irregularly shaped "rock" of beige clay. The goblin will be a humanlike character, but not quite human, which is why we don't just use flesh clay.

▼ **2** With your index finger and thumb, pinch the upper part of the rock, as shown. Make sure that you have a good amount of clay between your fingers, because we are going for a rather protuberant nose.

▼ **3** Here is what the shape roughly looks like after the nose extraction stage.

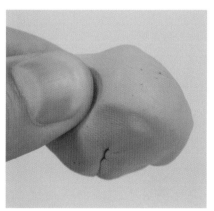

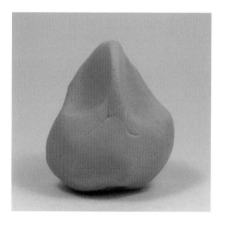

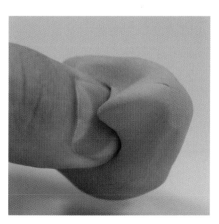

◀ **4** With your thumb, cut the nose where it stands out most to limit its length. Your thumbnail should create the flat surface under the nose where we will later put the nostrils.

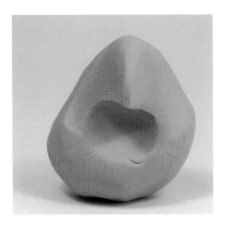

▲ **5** When you push with your thumb, do not stop when you reach the face. Push a little further until you create a small dent under the nose.

▲ **6** With your fingers, extract a neck out of the head, starting as shown. Gradually rotate the head, and repeat the procedure until you achieve an oblong protrusion by which you can hold the head while you work on it. It is this protrusion that will later help attach the head to the body.

Be careful not to compromise the volume of the lower part of the rock that we started with—the goblin will need to have a solid lower jaw.

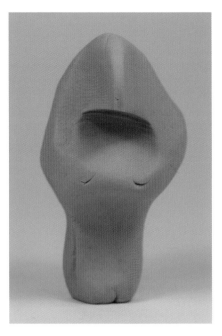

▲ **7** Here is the head and the neck of the future goblin so far.

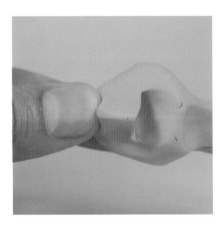

▲ **8** Limit the nose from the top with your finger.

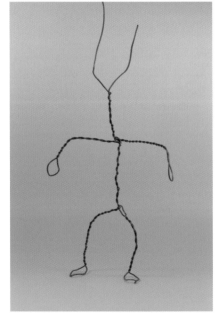

▲ **9** This is not an astronaut with two antennae but the wire outline you need to make for the armature. To complete the armature, twist every two opposite lines together until you create the "alien with two antennae" from the second picture. Finally, cut the recurring antennae off with your wire cutters.

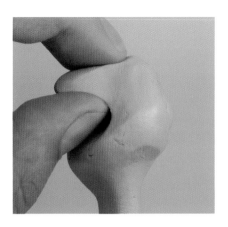

▲ **10** With your thumb under the nose and your index finger over it, as shown, gently pull to make the nose a little longer. As you push with your thumb at the very base of the nose, you will create two small bumps on both sides of the nose that we will later use to make the nostrils.

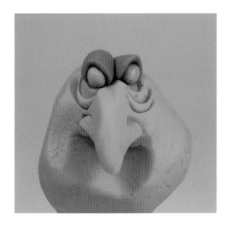

◀ **12** Then we rolled a small ball of light blue clay, and wrapped two-thirds of it in a flat piece of light brown clay to make the eyes. Next we put the eyes into the dents that had formed above the eye bags. We rotated each eye a little bit, so that the light brown bit of clay of one of the eyes, which fulfills the function of an eyelid, forms a right angle with the eyelid of the other eye. This right angle will give our goblin an intense and ferocious expression.

▲ **11** Here is the result of the steps that we have been practicing for some time now—making the bags under the eyes and the eyes themselves.

To create the bags under the goblin's eyes, we first pressed the tip of the cup-round clay shaper into the clay a few millimeters, down to the nose, to create a ripple of clay. Then we repeated the same action twice more, putting every consecutive ripple right above the previous one.

▲ **13** Use the tapered-point clay shaper to poke two deep holes for the goblin's nostrils until the outsides of the nostrils bulge a little bit. Then use the tip of the cup-round clay shaper to trace the outside of the nostrils, making sure to preserve the volume that you just gave them.

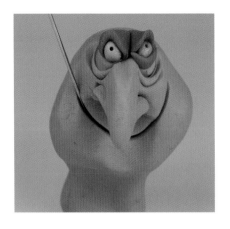

◀ **15** To finish the eyes, give them a third pair of eyelids of the same beige clay you used for the face. These new eyelids should cover some part of others under them, mostly the inner part (the one that is closer to the nose). Let the uppermost eyelids also form a right angle, contributing to the mean look of the critter.

The presence of eyelids reinforces the impression that the critter does, indeed, have something human to it (eyelids), but the number of eyelids indicates the opposite. Thus, a tension is palpable within the character, even a contradiction, which makes it all the more intriguing.

▲ **14** Poke two holes into the eyes to open them. Also, add two flat pieces of orange clay under the eyes as lower eyelids. Drive the needle deep into one of the cheeks, and draw the mouth of the goblin.

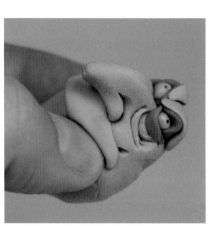

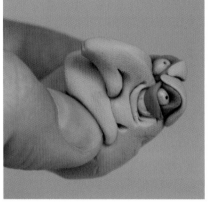

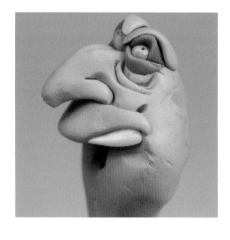

▲ **16** Using the clay shaper's handle, poke a hole in the middle of the goblin's mouth. Use a flat, oblong piece of clay to make the critter's upper lip, as shown.

▲ **17** Push up the right side of the upper lip with your thumb to make room for the teeth that you will insert soon.

▲ **18** Take a small flat piece of white or glow-in-the-dark polymer clay, and stick it underneath the upper lip, as shown. The goblin's grin will be asymmetric—only half of his teeth will show.

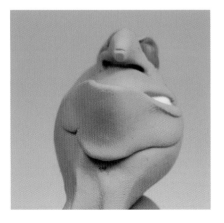

◀ **19** Make a flat piece of the beige clay that is wide in the middle and narrow toward the ends. Stick it on the pirate's face, as shown. The rim of this piece will serve as a lower lip. Leave a small opening in the middle between the lips, and allow the lower lip to protrude a little more than the upper one. Join the lips where the teeth start, but don't let the lower lip touch all of them—just the first one.

Use a needle to separate the individual teeth; cut into the white clay and drag toward the upper lip. Be careful not to leave marks on the upper lip.

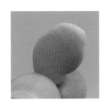

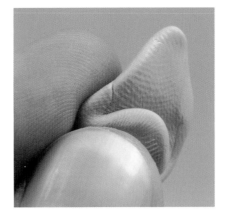

▲ **20** Roll a clay worm with a bulky middle and tapering ends. Bend it a little bit, and add it to the critter's face, as shown, to make a cheek. With the tip of a tapered-point clay shaper, smooth the lower end into the face. The upper end should be right above the nostril. Proceed similarly to make the other cheek.

▲ **21** Now for the ears. Make a flat, slightly elliptical piece of clay. Sharpen one end of it a little bit by squeezing it with your fingers, and fold the opposite end up, as shown.

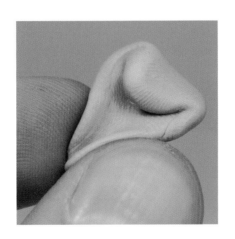

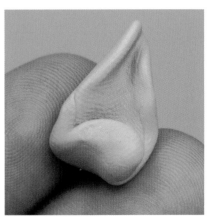

▶ **22** Fold the corners of the triangle inward, as shown. The objective here, as usual, is not to create an anatomically correct ear but to create an impression of an ear. In the case of the goblin, the weirder the ear looks, the better.

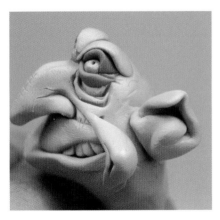

◀ **23** Stick the ear to the goblin's head. Notice that the shape in the picture was slightly distorted when we pushed it against the head. You should factor such distortion into the weirdness formula, too, and not seek to avoid or correct them.

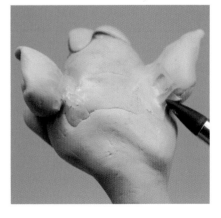

▲ **24** Using a tapered-point clay shaper, smudge the back of the ear into the critter's head to strengthen the bond with the head.

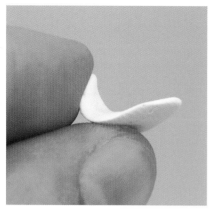

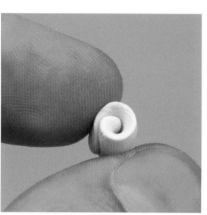

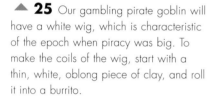

▲ **26** Stick the white burrito behind the ear of the goblin, just as you would stick a pencil behind yours. Make more coils, and distribute them on both sides of the head. In addition to making the goblin prettier, the coils will also strengthen the bond between the head and the ears.

▲ **25** Our gambling pirate goblin will have a white wig, which is characteristic of the epoch when piracy was big. To make the coils of the wig, start with a thin, white, oblong piece of clay, and roll it into a burrito.

▲ **28** Add an additional piece of beige clay over the tin foil to make the neck appear longer. The upper part of this piece should be firmly connected to the original neck.

▲ **27** The time has come to attach the goblin's head to his skeleton. Stick the head firmly on the wire that fulfills the function of the critter's neck. Be careful not to squish the face flat as you push down on the head.

Use generous amounts of tin foil to create the volume of the goblin's torso. Next, we will cover the armature with clay.

▲ **29** To make the goblin's Adam's apple, we use almost the same method as was used for the nose: Squeeze the throat between your index finger and thumb, cut horizontally with your thumb, and then squeeze again. To make the dent under the Adam's apple, simply push with the handle of the clay shaper.

Start covering the armature with dark blue clay. The critter will be wearing a long-sleeved shirt, and the only parts of "flesh" we will have to make in addition to his head and neck are the hands. Start covering the bare armature here and there to see where things are going.

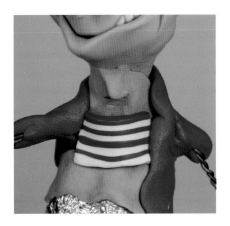

▲ **30** Our goblin will wear a blue-and-white-striped sailor shirt under his unbuttoned blue coat. Once again, the only part of the sailor shirt we have to make is the visible part. To create the stripes, alternate blue and white flat pieces of clay of the same thickness while laying them on top of each other. When the shirt becomes eight or ten layers thick, press the layers tightly together without overflattening them. Then use a sharp blade to slice them vertically. Make four or five slices. Cover the pirate's chest with the best one of them.

▲ **31** Cover the wire structure and the tin foil bottom of the critter with black clay. Whereas the layers of clay for the bottom can be thin, use a good, solid amount for the legs. Make the thighs thin, the knees bulkier, and the pant legs flared. Do not cover the wire legs all the way down to the feet, though; we will have to put the goblin's boots there.

▲ **32** You can see in the picture that we have put some more clay on the arms, too. We used blue clay, slightly darker than the blue stripes of the shirt. At this point we have established that if a darker blue is used for the coat, the contrast of the clothes will be better, so we decided to use the dark blue clay as the surface color for the coat.

▲ **33** Using dark brown clay, make the boots. Give the critter bigger heels so that he can be more stable. Once you finish the boots, make sure that the goblin can balance on his feet. You may have to adjust the position of his head and torso by making him stoop forward a little bit.

Place two small metallic circles on the goblin's boots, and pretend they look like buckles. You may have to use extra-strength glue to adhere them to the critter after baking.

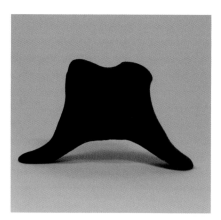

◀ **34** By now you are probably tired of playing with the legs, so let's go back to the head and give him a hat. Using black clay, make a shape like the one in the picture. This shape should be flat so that it doesn't weigh too much and so that the two lower ends of the hat can pass between the goblin's locks and his ears.

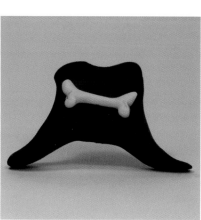

▲ **35** Make a bone of glow-in-the dark clay (like we did in the Skeleton lesson, see pages 95-96), and stick it horizontally to the front of the hat.

▲ **36** Attach the hat to the head, as shown, maximizing the contact surface between the black clay and the critter's head. The head is now almost finished. Enjoy the goblin's friendly smile.

▲ **37** Make a long, thin, wide strip of red clay, and wrap it around the critter's waist once or twice. This will be the exotic pirate's belt.

▲ **38** Add another slice of sailor shirt under the first one so that it covers the tin-foil tummy and part of the red belt. Then make the coat by covering all the parts of the critter's torso that should not be exposed with flat sheets of dark blue clay. Blend the sheets together with the tips of your fingers or a clay shaper.

▲ **39** Put the two smaller rings on one side of the goblin's coat to make buttons and a big earring through the lobe of his ear. Also, place a flat sheet of clay on the goblin's neck to make the coat's collar.

▲ **40** The only essential bit left to do is to give the goblin hands. Cover the wire loops at the ends of his arms with some beige clay, as shown, to make the palms of the hands.

▲ **41** Make a series of pointy fingers with big knuckles, and attach their thick ends firmly to the palms. Smudge the thick ends firmly into the palms.

▲ **42** Using a four-layered slice of sailor shirt, cover the spot where the fingers are attached to the palm. Then wrap an irregularly shaped cuff of dark blue clay around the wrist to strengthen the hand structure and make the connection with the arm.

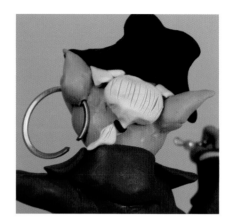

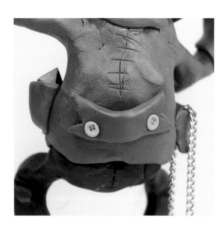

43 Make two sharp-angled triangles, and attach them to the coat, as shown, to make the goblin a little more sophisticated—he will be sporting "peaked lapels." Add two yellow clay circles to the buttons as well.

44 Bend a flat piece of dark blue clay a little, and attach it to the critter's coat to make a pocket. Using the tapered-point clay shaper, make the pocket's edges stick firmly to the coat. Draw the stitches that supposedly hold it there with the needle. Mark four holes in a square formation on each button.

45 Turn the critter around, and make the back part of his wig. It should consist of a bulky upper part and a tiny ponytail. Put a small piece of black clay in the base of the ponytail to keep the hairs together. Using the pin, draw some individual hairs.

47 We are approaching the end of this lesson, so, as usual, it is time to draw with the needle. Draw deep dimples on the pirate's cheeks. Add a series of dots on his upper lip as if he is unshaven. Draw some stitches on his nose—it is not without a fight that the pirate made his fortune!

46 And back to haute couture again—make a shape like the one in the picture to make the back belt of the coat. Add two yellow buttons. Make stitches with the needle in the center of the back. Make the other pocket, poking a hole in it so that a piece of chain can hang loosely from there.

48 Put a piece of a pearl necklace in the goblin's hands, and close his fingers firmly around it. Use all the little treasures you can find to put in the goblin's pockets, teeth, or hands. We found a rhinestone that fit nicely into his right pocket.

49 Flatten the tip of the boots to give the critter more style.

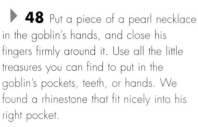

◀ **50** Here is the finished gambling goblin pirate! Notice that we used two dice to complete the whole picture. The dice are already cast, showing our goblin is not a static character—he has just performed an action. The dice, which are not part of the figure itself, turn out to be an integral part of it.

Bake the goblin following the clay manufacturer's instructions, and let him cool. Consider baking him horizontally, on some tin-foil cushions.

For more tips on baking, see page 7.

Variation Idea
Roman Character

This Roman character is made using a maximum of non-clay objects and part of a regular hen's feather. The interesting thing about him is that he is not even an advanced character—and he even gets to be the last critter in this book. To make his legs, I used the single-limb armature we practiced in the Trutlio the Troll lesson. The torso, head, and arms were made following the principles of the Knight in Shining Armor lesson.

How Far Can and Should Critter-Making Go?
Working on Details and Making Stories with Your Characters

Critter-making can go very far; one is either tempted to go into the most minute details of a critter or get caught up in making an intricate set to provide a context for the character they have created. Putting your italicized initials on every gray hair on your goblin's head would be an example of the former, and making a highway that leads to the castle where your knight dwells in the middle of a forest, on an island, in a sea, on a planet, in a universe in a parallel polymer-clay dimension would be an example of the latter. As you can see, even the very sentence that describes the process of going to these two extremes is long and confusing.

Of course, going to extremes can be a lot of fun and is definitely worth trying at some point, but do not forget that there is a middle road you should explore:

When the random passerby looks at your creation, the character's highlights should be more or less apparent, and only then should there be enough detail to keep the viewer's interest for a while. It is better, for example, to spend more time giving a creature a big crooked nose and a huge unibrow than to meticulously put all the 365 stitches that it usually takes to fasten a patch on a sleeve.

By analogy, a finished character should be expressive enough on its own to stimulate the onlooker's imagination. Making an auxiliary setting may provide the context, but that context should be first and foremost suggested in the character itself. Let us take the Gambling Goblin Pirate lesson, for example: The dice we used in this final project confirmed he was a gambler, but it was you who created the grinning goblin and the greedy pirate.

If you followed all the lessons in this book you may have built a whole cast of characters with which to stage your own fairy tale. Take advantage of the fact that many of the characters are compatible—you can make a knight on a horse fighting a dragon, a wizard with a raven (the generic bird, in black) perched on his shoulder, a Santa with a helper elf and a reindeer (using the horse lesson and the armature technique for the antlers), a clumsy troll with a bird on his head…you get the idea. Here is an example:

Sir George Tickles the Dragon

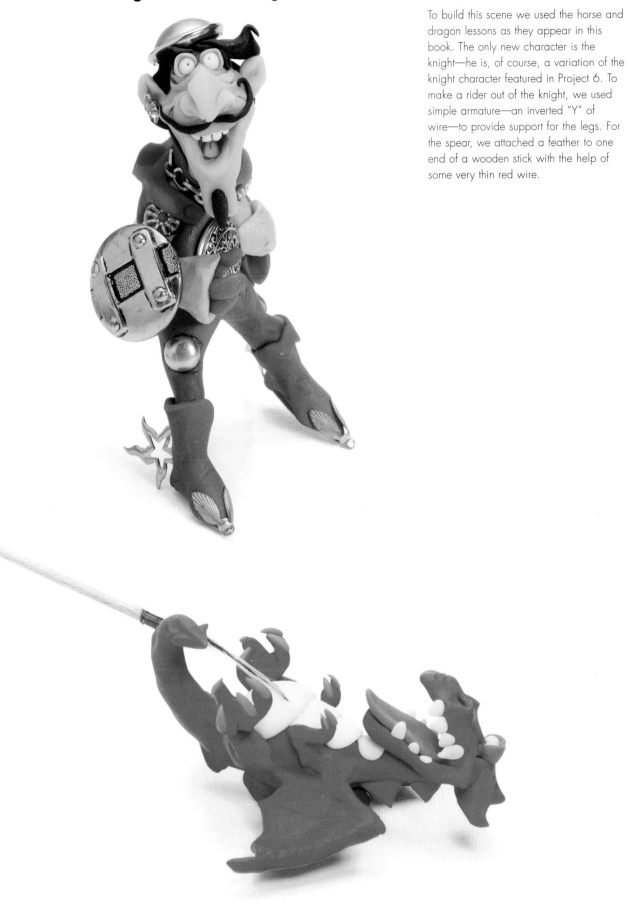

To build this scene we used the horse and dragon lessons as they appear in this book. The only new character is the knight—he is, of course, a variation of the knight character featured in Project 6. To make a rider out of the knight, we used simple armature—an inverted "Y" of wire—to provide support for the legs. For the spear, we attached a feather to one end of a wooden stick with the help of some very thin red wire.

Information on Polymer Clay

Polymer Clay Central
www.polymerclaycentral.com
The biggest Internet portal dedicated to polymer clay art: A great online resource for beginners and advanced clayers alike—a treasury of all kinds of polymer clay-related information. PCC's forum is a meeting place for many artists of the international polymer clay community.

Polymer Clay, Tools, and Supplies

Australia
Staedtler (Pacific) Pty Ltd.
P.O. Box 576, 1 Inman Road
Dee Why, NSW 2099
phone: 2-9982-4555
Fimo

Rossdale Pty Ltd.
137 Noone Street, Clifton Hills
VIC 3068
Premo, Sculpey

Bulgaria
Marnie Ltd.
Bul. "Tzarigradsko chossee"
Office 608, 7 km
1784 Sofia
marnie.bg@dir.bg
Fimo, Fimo Soft

United Kingdom
Fimo and Fimo Soft polymer clays are generally the easiest to find in Europe. To locate your local retail agent visit the Fimo manufacturer go to www.eberhardfaber.de

American Art Clay Co. Inc.
P.O. Box 467
Longton
Stoke-On-Trent, ST3 7DN
phone: 44-01782-399219
fax: 44-01782-394891
andrewcarter@amaco.uk.co
www.amaco.uk.co
General supplies, push molds, tools

Homecrafts Direct
P.O. Box 247
Leicester, LE1 9QS
phone: 44-0116-251-0405
post@speccrafts.co.uk
www.speccrafts.co.uk
General supplies, Formello, tools

The Polymer Clay Pit
www.polymerclaypit.co.uk
General supplies

Organizations

United States

Accent Import Export, Inc.
1501 Loveridge Road, Box 16
Pittsburg, CA 94565
phone: 1-800-989-2889
sean@fimozone.com
www.fimozone.com
General supplies, tools, books

American Art Clay Co., Inc.
4717 West 16th Street
Indianapolis, IN 46222
phone: 1-800-374-1600
fax: 317-248-9300
catalog@amaco.com
www.amaco.com
General supplies, tools

Clay Factory, Inc.
P.O. Box 460598
Escondido, CA 92046-0598
phone: 877-728-5739
clayfactoryinc@clayfactoryinc.com
www.clayfactoryinc.com
General supplies, Premo, Sculpey,
Super Sculpey, Sculpey111, Super Flex

Mindstorm Productions, Inc.
2625 Alcatraz Avenue, Suite 241 1
Berkeley, CA 94705
phone: 510-644-1952
fax: 510-644-3910
burt@mindstorm-inc.com
www.mindstorm-inc.com
Instructional videos

Polymer Clay Express
13017 Wisteria Drive, Box 275
Germantown, MD 20874
phone: 1-800-844-0138
fax: 301-482-0610
www.polymerclayexpress.com
General supplies, hard-to-find items

Prairie Craft Company
P.O. Box 209
Florissant, CO 80816-0209
phone: 1-800-779-0615
fax: 719-748-5112
vernon@pcisys.net
www.prairiecraft.com
General supplies, tools

Organizations

New Zealand

New Zealand Polymer Clay Guild
8 Cherry Place
Casebrook
Christchurch 8005
phone/fax: 0064-3-359-2989
www.zigzag.co.nz/NZPCG/

United Kingdom

The British Polymer Clay Guild
48 Park Close
Hethersett
Norwich, Norfolk NR9 3EW
www.polymerclaypit.co.uk/polyclay/
  guild/britpol.htm

United States

National Polymer Clay Guild
PMB 345
1350 Beverly Road, 115
McLean, VA 22101
www.npcg.org

ACKNOWLEDGMENTS

Many thanks to my family and my parents, Irina Tilova and Ustinian Tilov, without whose love and encouragement none of this would have been possible.

Many thanks to my friends Leigh and Stephen Ross, who have always supported my clay adventures through the years and have been there for me.

Many thanks to Mary Ann Hall of Rockport Publishers and to the whole team for their patience and enthusiasm in working with me on this project.

ABOUT THE AUTHOR

Dinko Tilov has been creating amazing 3 to 5 inch (8 cm to 13 cm) creatures using polymer clay and mixed media ever since he was a child. His unique characters have been featured on polymer clay websites, in newsletters, galleries, and in a calendar. He has lived and studied in Bulgaria (where he is from), France, and the United States, where he is currently in his senior year at Reed College. Much of his prolific work can be viewed at his website: www.dinkos.com.